GENERAL PROGRESS PAPERS

ANSWER BOOK

WRITTEN BY H H THOMAS   REVISED BY A J THOMAS

Nelson

Preface

It was with great trepidation and humility that I approached the revision of this series, which has been continuously in print and used by children for thirty-five years, with sales exceeding ten million copies.

I have tried to preserve the spirit and flavour of the original books, while altering them to reflect the immense changes in our society in the intervening years. The series was intended to "teach by doing" rather than to serve only as test material. I have tried to continue that principle and to extend it.

I have received an enormous amount of help. Above all I am indebted to my wife, Myrna. Her help has been invaluable. In addition to contributing a large amount of the new material, she has been a constant source of inspiration and ideas. I am also indebted to my daughters, Lisa, Sara and Mary, for many valuable suggestions, to my brother Dr. C.W. Thomas for his constructive criticism of the revised manuscripts, and to the many others who have helped me but are too numerous to name.

With so much help of quality, any failings in this revised series rest solely on my own inadequacy.

AJT

Notes to teachers and parents

1. This series of papers is designed to help measure the progress of children between the ages of 10 and 12. It also aims to *develop* their reasoning and problem-solving skills.
2. The very able pupil who has practised thoroughly might be expected to attain a high score when 45 minutes is allowed for a complete paper.
3. These papers should prove of equal value to the less able or less experienced pupil who can benefit greatly from practice and exposure to problem-solving. These children should be given much more time to deal with the questions and allowed to explore some of the questions at leisure. They should not be discouraged if they are slow to start with; speed will come with familiarity and understanding with practice. Even when the pupil cannot solve a particular problem after some time, he/she should be encouraged to look at the answer and then try to work out how it should have been done.
4. In marking, one mark is allowed for each answer and that answer is normally the standard answer in the Answer Book. It is inevitable, however, that an occasional question should have an alternative answer which is as valid as the one given. In this case discretion should be used. A lively debate about the validity of an answer is likely to teach a great deal.

Instructions to pupils

(i) One mark is allowed for each answer.
(ii) Read each question most carefully to be sure that you fully understand it.
(iii) Pupils should learn to follow instructions precisely. Failure to do so frequently loses candidates many marks in school or public examinations. Note the following points in particular.

   a If asked to cross out certain words, the pupil should do so by drawing a single black line through the words and not cross out anything else.
   b If a pupil is asked to put a ring round a word or underline a word, this should be done and nothing else.
   c Sometimes the question requires that *one* word should be underlined, and sometimes *two* words. Care should be taken to do exactly what is asked.
   d Answers must be placed in the spaces allowed for them, and not in the margin or any other odd space that happens to be there.

If these instructions seem to be rather fussy, remember that in school or public examinations, examiners have a very large number of papers to mark and they do not have the time to search for the answers or judge whether the candidate knew the right answer but wrote it incorrectly. *Get used to being precise and scoring all the marks of which you are capable.*

A.J.T.

PAPER 1

[1–3]
In each of the following sentences, underline the word or phrase in brackets which completes the sentence correctly.

1. I am 3 years older than Martin who was born in 1977. I was therefore born in (1978, <u>1974</u>, 1973, 1975).

2. Sara had 22p more than I had, and I had 17p. Sara therefore had (45p, 5p, <u>39p</u>, 9p).

3. I can walk at the rate of 4 kilometres an hour. Nicholas can walk a kilometre an hour faster than I can. He can therefore walk a kilometre in (10, 11, <u>12</u>, 13, 15) minutes.

[4–13]
In each of the following groups of words, underline the word that means the opposite of the word in heavy type, and put a ring round the word that means the same.

4–5	**mend**	tear	stocking	(repair)	damage	renew
6–7	**climb**	tree	(ascend)	mountain	fall	<u>descend</u>
8–9	**help**	helpful	harm	(aid)	injure	<u>hinder</u>
10–11	**happy**	laughing	(glad)	crying	<u>sad</u>	delighted
12–13	**enemy**	hostile	helper	(foe)	<u>friend</u>	love

[14–20]
Here is an addition and a subtraction with some figures missed out. Dots take the place of figures. Write the missing figures where the dots are.

14–17
```
  7538
  2496
  4654
  3825
 -----
 18513
```

18–20
```
  565
  389
  ---
  176
```

[21–25]
In my class are five friends: **A, B, C, D** and **E**.
A, D and **E** are tall; the others are short. **D, B** and **E** are fair; the others are dark. **B, C** and **E** wear glasses.
Now complete the following sentences:

21. In the front desk sits ......**B**......, a short fair boy with glasses.

22. Behind him sits ......**D**...... who is tall and fair, and does not wear glasses.

23. On his right we see ......**E**...... sitting. She is tall and fair and wears glasses.

24 On his left there sits ......**C**......, a short dark girl with glasses.

25 How would you describe the fifth friend?
......**Tall,**......, ...**dark,**......, ...**without glasses**......

[26–30]
Look at this example: **hand** is to **glove** as **foot** is to **boot**. There is a likeness because a boot covers a foot as a glove covers a hand. Now complete the following sentences by underlining the correct word in brackets:

26 **fat** is to **thin** as **large** is to (thick, <u>small</u>, tall, big)

27 **fox** is to **cub** as **horse** is to (calf, mare, <u>foal</u>, stallion)

28 **bus** is to **road** as **ship** is to (water, air, desert, <u>sea</u>)

29 **sad** is to **tears** as **happy** is to (joy, glad, <u>smile</u>, happiness)

30 **arm** is to **elbow** as **door** is to (knob, lock, <u>hinge</u>, post)

[31–35]
Look at the words below. If a word contains both **i** and **e** put the number **1** on the dotted line. If it contains **i** but not **e** put **2**; if **e** but not **i** put **3**; if neither **i** nor **e** put **4**; if both twice put **5**.

31 frail ......**2**......   32 experimenting ......**5**......

33 offend ......**3**......   34 friends ......**1**......   35 float ......**4**......

[36–40]
Look at these numbers: **6 8 10 12 14 (16)**
16 has been put in brackets because the other numbers have been increased 2 at a time so that after **14** you must have **16**. Write in brackets the number that should come next in each line.

36 1   6   11   16   21   (......**26**......)
37 9   13   18   24   31   39   (......**48**......)
38 7680   768   76·8   7·68   ·768   (......**·0768**......)
39 2   4   16   (......**256**......)
40 2   4   8   16   32   (......**64**......)

[41–45]
In each of the following lines, underline the word that does not fit in with the others.

41 touch   taste   smell   <u>recognise</u>   see   hear
42 train   bus   taxi   <u>ship</u>   car   lorry
43 <u>William</u> Kim   Amy   Tara   Lucy   Laura
44 Belgium   Holland   France   <u>Egypt</u>   Italy   Spain
45 football   cricket   <u>snooker</u>   hockey   polo   tennis

[46–51]
Underline the name of the smallest item on each line and put a ring around the name of the largest:

46–47   second   week   minute   hour   day   (month)

48–49   (library)   shelf   book   word   line   page

50–51   3649   4369   3469   3864   9346   (9643)

[52–54]

52   Write the most frequent letter in the word **accommodation**. ......o......

53   Give the letter which occurs twice in **idleness** and only once in **beautiful**.

......e......

54   If you had as many pounds as there are letters **a** in the word **accommodation** and bought 5 chocolate bars at 25p each, how much change would you get? ......75p......

[55–58]
Underline the general word in each of the following groups.

55   swallow   duck   cock   bird   sparrow   owl

56   city   London   Bristol   Manchester   Leeds   Liverpool

57   cod   plaice   herring   halibut   fish   whiting

58   potato   pea   cabbage   cauliflower   bean   vegetable

[59–62]
Here are the populations of a number of British towns:

Cardiff	286,000	Cambridge	106,000	Chester	117,000
Pembroke	10,000	Romford	78,000	Canterbury	36,000
Rhyl	23,000	Ross-on-Wye	6,000		

59   Which town has the largest population? ......Cardiff......

60   Which town has 6 times as many people as Ross-on-Wye?

......Canterbury......

61   Which town has a population equal to that of Rhyl, Romford, Pembroke and Ross-on-Wye combined? ......Chester......

62   How many towns have fewer than 40,000 inhabitants? ......Four......

63   If 4 is subtracted from 3 times a certain number, the answer is 23. What is the number? ......9......

PAPER 1

[64–67]
Sara and Natalie each have a watch. Sara's watch is a quartz watch and keeps good time, but Natalie's watch gains 3 minutes every hour. They set both watches at 1000 hours.

64 What will be the time by Natalie's watch at 1500 hours? ...... **1515 hrs** ......

65 When Natalie's watch says 2030 hours, what is the time by Sara's?

...... **2000 hrs** ......

66 When it is 1820 hours by Sara's watch, what time does Natalie's show?

...... **1845 hrs** ......

67 How many minutes' difference will there be in the times shown by the two watches at 2240 hours? ...... **38 mins** ......

68–69 Two boys, Robert and Ashley, each own some books. If Ashley sold two to Robert they would both have the same number of books. If Robert sold two books to Ashley then he would have half as many as Ashley. How many books does each boy own?

Robert ...... **10** ......   Ashley ...... **14** ......

[70–74]
Look at this example: **8** is to **9** as **10** is to (9 **11** 12 14)
The number has been underlined because it is one more than **10**, just as **9** is one more than **8**.
Complete the following by underlining the correct answers:

70 **ab** is to **cd** as **hi** is to (ef gh **jk** lm op)

71 **67** is to **76** as **89** is to (87 78 **98** 76)

72 **74** is to **93** as **29** is to (37 43 56 **48** 39)

73 **35** is to **17** as **36** is to (27 **18** 19 23 53)

74 **jhi** is to **ihj** as **qpo** is to (qpo poq **opq** jhi)

[75–79]
In each of the following sentences the letters of the first word are mixed up. What is the word?
Example: **erbda** is something we eat. The correct word is **bread**.

75 **trubet** is something we often eat on sandwiches   ...... **butter** ......

76 **slump** are fruit which grow on trees   ...... **plums** ......

77 **fifarge** is a wild grazing animal   ...... **giraffe** ......

78 **sayid** is a common wild flower   ...... **daisy** ......

79 **ramoyces** is a common tree with interesting seeds   ...... **sycamore** ......

80 Twice **a** is 3 times **b**. If **b** = 8 what does **a** represent?   ...... **12** ......

[81–84]
I have nine balls that I number **1** to **9**. Numbers **1, 4** and **7** are red; **3, 5** and **8** are green; the rest are black.
Numbers **2, 5** and **7** are large; **1, 4** and **9** are medium size; the rest are small.

81 I want a large red ball. Which number is it? ....7............

82 I want a small black ball. Which number is it? ....6............

83 I want a medium black ball. Which number is it? ....9............

84 I want a small green ball. Which number is it? ....3 or 8............

85 Which was the largest island in the Pacific Ocean before Australia was discovered? ....Australia........

[86–90]
My house is medium sized and costs £400 to heat in an average year. I want to reduce this cost as far as possible. I am advised that 20% of the heat is lost through the windows and 40% through the roof. Double glazing will save half of the heat lost through the windows and will cost £2000. Insulating the roof will cost £480 and save three-quarters of the heat lost through the roof.

86 How much will double glazing save each year? ....£40........

87 How much will roof insulation save each year? ....£120........

88 How many years will it take to recover the cost of double glazing?
........50........

89 How many years will it take to recover the cost of roof insulation?
........4........

90 Which would you advise me to have done? ....Roof insulation........

[91–95]
Imagine you have done the following sums on your electronic calculator. Without actually using a calculator, if you think the answers are right, tick them; if you think they are wrong put a cross beside the answer.

91 489 × 3·17 = 1550·13 ....✓........

92 101 + 214 + 107 + 98 + 189 = 1709 ....+........

93 3789 × 1·34 = 2827·612 ....+........

94 1022 + 1231 − 212 = 2041 ....✓........

95 If you think any of the sums are wrong, underline the most probable reason: the calculator is broken, the batteries are low, <u>figures or signs were entered incorrectly</u>.

[96–100]

96 A person who designs houses or other buildings is called an <u>architect</u>

97 At the checkout in a supermarket a <u>cashier</u> collects your money.

98 A house is painted by a <u>decorator</u>

99 Planes are told where to fly by an <u>air</u> <u>traffic</u> <u>controller</u>

100 To help ships find their way they employ a <u>navigator</u>

PAPER 2

[1–4]

1. Underline any letters that occur more than twice in the word **sens<u>i</u>b<u>i</u>l<u>i</u>ty**.

2. Number the following according to size starting with **1**:

   ......5...... cat ......4...... mouse ......2...... ant ......7...... horse

   ......6...... lion ......3...... bee ......1...... flea

3. Twice **a** equals 3 times **b**, and half of **b** equals **c**. If **c** equals 6, what does **a** equal? ......18......

4. My father is three times as old as I am. I am 12. How many times older than I, was he 4 years ago? ......4 times......

[5–10]
In the following pairs of words some mean almost the same while others are quite different in meaning, and yet other pairs are exact opposites. For pairs of words similar in meaning write **S**; if different write **D**; and if opposite write **O**.

5. big–little ......O......
6. idle–lazy ......S......
7. intelligent–happy ......D......
8. rich–wealthy ......S......
9. friendly–hostile ......O......
10. pair–pear ......D......

[11–13]
Cross out the unwanted part of a word in each sentence:

11. These wild flowers grow everywhere; they are very ~~un~~common.
12. He ordered a cab~~bage~~ and drove to the station in it.
13. The red rose is the ~~cauli~~flower of the House of Lancaster.

14–15 Put a ring round each correct sum:

$9 \times 8 = 56$ $9 \times 0 = 90$ $9 + 8 = 72$
(⚬ $9 \times 7 = 63$ ⚬) $9 + 7 = 18$ (⚬ $3 \times \frac{6}{2} = 9$ ⚬)

[16–17]
Arrange these words in the two sentences below, putting similar meanings together:

second   minute   small   third

16. **second** and ......third...... go together.
17. ......minute...... and ......small...... go together.

[18–21]
Write the opposite of these words:

18 foolish .... wise ....   19 failure .... success ....

20 gather .... scatter ....   21 proud .... humble ....

[22–23]

22–23 Cross out the two unsuitable words in each of the two groups so that the sentence makes sense:
It is usually thought that accidents are caused/~~avoided~~/~~increased~~ by cars travelling too fast/~~town~~/~~slowly~~/~~slippery~~.

[24–25]
This square is divided into 16 equal parts.

24 What fraction of the whole square is shaded? .... $\frac{1}{2}$ ....

25 If I shaded two more small squares what fraction of the whole square would then be shaded? .... $\frac{5}{8}$ ....

[26–31]
Complete the sentences by underlining the correct word in the brackets:

26 **joy** is to **sorrow** as **plentiful** is to (much, little, <u>scarce</u>, cry, tears)
27 **east** is to **west** as **slowly** is to (walk, <u>quickly</u>, run, loiter, rapid)
28 **poem** is to **poet** as (writer, author, story, <u>novel</u>, comic) is to **novelist**
29 (round, <u>four</u>, regular, two) is to **square** as **three** is to **triangle**
30 **sight** is to **eye** as **odour** is to (hear, ear, smell, scent, <u>nose</u>)
31 **height** is to **mountain** as (swift, deep, broad, <u>length</u>, rapid) is to **river**

[32–36]
Put a ring around the word that includes most of the others and cross out the words that do not fit in with the rest.

coal   coke   ~~warmth~~   petrol   ~~fire~~   oil

paraffin   ~~steam~~   ~~stove~~   wood   gas   (fuel)

[37–44]
Read these lines of words. Some words are in the wrong lines.

unit	ten	milligram	year
millimetre	centimetre	week	kilometre
day	kilogram	hundred	month
tonne	metre	thousand	gram

Here are some of the same words, now in the correct lines. Fill in the others in their proper places.

	unit	ten	hundred	thousand
37	millimetre	38 centimetre	39 metre	40 kilometre
	day	41 week	42 month	year
43	milligram	gram	kilogram	44 tonne

45 Three young people are at a disco in Paris. James can speak English, German and French, Adeline can speak French and German, and Helga can speak Dutch and German. Can they carry on a conversation? Underline your choice.
(a) <u>Yes</u> (b) No (c) I cannot tell from the piece

[46–49]
Write in the brackets the numbers that have been left out:

46 9   13   17   21   (25)   29   31
47 36   30   24   18   (12)
48 4   9   14   15   20   25   (26)   31
49 15   13   11   9   11   13   (15)   13

[50–51]
50 A man walks 5 km east, then 5 km south, then 5 km west. How far is he from where he started? 5 km

51 In which direction will he walk home? Underline the correct answer.
<u>north</u>   south   east   west

PAPER 2

[52–57]
In a line ready to come into school stood David, Daniel, Louise, Linda and James, one behind the other but not in this order. They all stood behind Rebecca who was first in line because she was the tallest. They stood in order of height and as Louise was the shortest she was last. Daniel stood behind David but in front of Linda. James was shorter than Daniel and Linda.

52 How many children were shorter than Rebecca? *5*

53 How many stood between David and James? *2*

54 How many were taller than Linda? *3*

55 Who stood immediately in front of James? *Linda*

56 Who was the second tallest boy in the line? *Daniel*

57 David stood between *Rebecca* and *Daniel*

58 Fill in the last number in the series.
    3   9   27   81   243   *729*

59 If **a** = 1, **b** = 2, **c** = 3 etc., what figures would stand for the word **ideal**?
    9 4 5 1   12

[60–61]
This sentence has been written twice. Cross out words or parts of words so that it makes sense. Then cross out different words or parts of words to give it different sense.

60 She was very unhappy when her mother ~~came back and~~ went away.

61 She was very ~~un~~happy when her mother came back ~~and went away~~.

62 It is 1702 hours. What time would you think it was if you mistook the long hand of the clock for the short hand? *1225 hrs*

[63–65]
Put in the missing signs in these sums:

63 19 + 3 *÷* 11 = 2   64 7 *×* 6 = 42

65 25p *÷* 5 = 5p

[66–68]
Underline the correct answers to the following:

66 All trees have: nests   flowers   fruit   <u>roots</u>   <u>branches</u>

67 All houses have: tenants furniture <u>foundations</u> <u>windows</u> garages

68 All flowers have: scent   <u>petals</u>   bees   leaves   seeds

[69–71]
Complete the following by putting in the correct word:

69 **coming** is to **going** as **arrival** is to ....*departure*........

70 **body** is to **blood** as **tree** is to ....*sap*........

71 **always** is to **never** as ....*everything*........ is to **nothing**

[72–73]
Brown and Jones are fair. Smith and Davies are dark. Brown and Davies are tall. Smith and Jones are short.

72 Who is tall and fair? ....*Brown*........

73 Who is short and dark? ....*Smith*........

[74–80]
On your breakfast table you might find the following things. The words have been jumbled so that although all the letters are correct they are in the wrong order. What are the things?

74 redab ....*bread*........

75 gropride ....*porridge*........

76 lakfrocsen ....*cornflakes*........

77 satto ....*toast*........

78 fofece ....*coffee*........

79 alarmedam ....*marmalade*........

80 guars ....*sugar*........

[81–92]
Below are three world weather forecasts taken from the same newspaper on different dates.

(A)	Temp. °C	°F	Weather	(B)	Temp. °C	°F	Weather
Athens	22	72	Sunny	Athens	33	91	Sunny
Cape Town	19	67	Fair	Cape Town	14	57	Fair
Lisbon	16	61	Cloudy	Lisbon	27	81	Sunny
London	14	57	Rain	London	25	78	Sunny
Moscow	16	61	Fair	Moscow	29	85	Bright
New York	20	69	Sunny	New York	34	93	Thunder
Singapore	32	88	Heavy showers	Singapore	32	89	Cloudy
Sydney	17	63	Sunny	Sydney	13	55	Rain
Tokyo	18	64	Sunny	Tokyo	27	81	Fair
Wellington	12	53	Showers	Wellington	44	39	Rain

(C)	Temp. °C	°F	Weather
Athens	9	48	Rain
Cape Town	27	81	Sunny
Lisbon	5	41	Fog
London	1	34	Snow showers
Moscow	−27	−17	Snow
New York	−8	18	Bright
Singapore	30	87	Rain
Sydney	33	91	Sunny
Tokyo	−2	28	Fair
Wellington	24	76	Sunny

Which weather forecast appeared on:

81 June 3rd? .... A .... **82** Jan 28th? .... C ....
83 Aug 12th? .... B ....

84–87 Name four of the cities other than London which are capitals of their country. .... Athens .... Moscow ....
.... Lisbon .... Tokyo ....

From these patterns of weather can you identify:

88–89 Two cities in the lists which are in the southern hemisphere?
.... Sydney .... Wellington or Cape Town ....

90 Which city lies close to the equator? .... Singapore ....
91 Which city is the most northerly? .... Moscow ....
92 Which city is the southernmost? .... Wellington ....

[93–100]

You are invited to visit Scarborough, on a sunny day in late November. You are sent a street plan of the town. You arrive at the railway station at midday. The entrance to the station is on Valley Bridge Road. Your instructions tell you to go north up Valley Bridge Road.

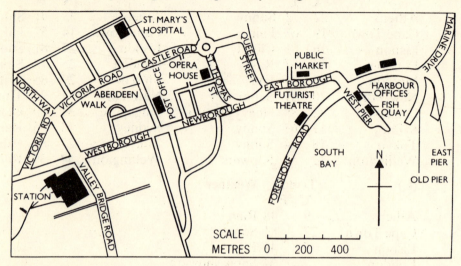

93 The sun will be: in your eyes, on your left shoulder, <u>on the back of your neck.</u> Underline the correct answer.
Take the first right turn and the second left.

94 After walking 120 metres up this road what building will be on your right?
...... **Post Office** ......
Turn right at the end of this road and go in a north-easterly direction until you come to a roundabout. Turn until the sun is in your eyes and walk on for about 150 metres.

95 What building will now be on your right? ...... **Opera House** ......
Continue in the same direction until you come to Newborough. Turn east.

96 Just after the second left turn there is a large building on your left. What is it?
...... **Public Market** ......
Continue walking in the same direction following the road round a righthand curve.

97 You are then facing the ...... **West Pier** ......
Proceed south-east along it.

98 You pass the ...... **Harbour Offices** ......
and about 50 metres later

99 the ...... **Fish Quay** ......

100 What will happen if you continue to walk in the same direction?
...... **I will fall in the sea** ......

PAPER 3

1. Cross out the eighth word in this sentence:
   He was the eighth boy to be ~~awarded~~ his swimming badge.

2. If a bricklayer can build a wall 30 metres long and 1.5 metres high in 16 hours, and he is joined by a second bricklayer of equal competence when the wall is half finished, how long will the building of the wall take altogether? ......12 hrs......

3. How many leaves are there on a tree in winter? Underline the correct answer.
   (a) None   (b) Trees are bare in winter   (c) <u>It depends on the kind of tree</u>

4. One day of the week begins with the fourth letter after **s** in the alphabet. Write down the third letter of the name of that day. ......d......

5. Which letter in the word **Saturday** comes latest in the alphabet?
   ......y......

[6–10]
Look at the drawing and answer the following questions:

6. What numbers are in the rectangle and the triangle? ......1, 2......
7. What numbers are in the rectangle and the circle? ......1, 3......
8. What number is in the rectangle, circle and triangle? ......1......
9. What numbers are in the triangle but not the circle? ......2, 4......
10. What number is in the rectangle but not in the circle or triangle? ......6......

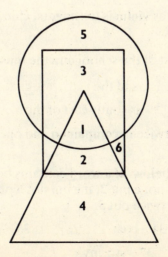

PAPER 3

[11–20]
One word has been left out of each line in the following passage. These spaces have been marked with a cross. Write in the space at the end of the line what you think the word should be.

11 Plants require soil, moisture, x and food. ..... light .....
12 One of the x difficult problems of home plant ..... most .....
13 growers is knowing x to water and how much. ..... when .....
14 A moisture meter is x answer to this problem. ..... one/an .....
15 Just insert the probe to the level of the x ..... roots .....
16 and the meter will indicate to you how x the ..... moist .....
17 soil is around the roots x is where moisture ..... which .....
18 is best x by the plant. Different plants need ..... used/absorbed .....
19 different amounts of moisture to x best. Some ..... grow .....
20 need a lot of water; x prefer the soil almost dry. ..... others .....

[21–27]
Complete these statements by underlining the correct word in the brackets:

21 **arm** is to **elbow** as **leg** is to (foot, <u>knee</u>, sinew, joint)
22 **multiply** is to **divide** as **add** is to (sum, arithmetic, <u>subtract</u>, total)
23 **multiply** is to **divide** as **large** is to (subtract, big, <u>small</u>, great)
24 **coat** is to **cloth** as **tyre** is to (<u>rubber</u>, cover, bicycle, wheel)
25 **first** is to **last** as **head** is to (horse, race, prize, <u>tail</u>)
26 **violin** is to **string** as **piano** is to (hammer, key, <u>wire</u>)
27 **piano** is to **hammer** as **violin** is to (fingers, chin, <u>bow</u>)

[28–31]
The park is due west of the school and the museum is due north of the park.

28–29 The ..... school ..... and the ..... museum ..... are farthest apart.
30–31 The ..... school ..... is south-east of the ..... museum .....

32 What letter comes twice in **companion** and once in **friendship**? ..... n .....

[33–37]
Look at the words below. If a word contains both **a** and **e** put **1** on the dotted line; if **a** but not **e** put **2**; if **e** but not **a** put **3**; if neither **a** nor **e** put **4**; and if **a** or **e** comes twice put **5**.

33 friend ..... 3 .....   34 coat ..... 2 .....   35 great ..... 1 .....
36 feathers ..... 5 .....   37 stormy ..... 4 .....

— PAPER 3 —

[38–44]
Fill in the missing figures in these two sums.

38–41
```
   6.945
  76.82
  6398
  ─────
  21025
```

42–44
```
   663
   47.6
   ───
   187
```

[45–48]

45 Half of **x** is 2.5 times 4. What is **x**? .... 20 ....

46 Twice **a** is three times 6. What is **a**? .... 9 ....

47 How much is twice the half of 237? .... 237 ....

48 **c** is three times **a** and twice **b**. If **b** − **a** = 2, what is **c**? .... 12 ....

[49–50]
A straight street has eight street lamps. If each pair are 20 metres apart, how far is it from the first to the last? .... 140 metres ....

[51–62]
Here is a list of ordinary return train fares from Newton, Highville and Blackford to a number of local stations. The amount of the fare depends on the length of the journey.

To	From Newton	From Highville	From Blackford
Newton	—	£5.60	£6.90
Easton	£5.50	£6.30	£7.00
Northbury	£2.70	£4.80	£4.10
Canfield	£6.00	£8.10	£2.70
Oldcastle	£8.20	£6.40	£8.00
Minster	£5.30	£1.45	£1.70

51–52 Which is the shortest journey?

.... Highville .... to .... Minster ....

53–54 Which is the longest journey?

.... Newton .... to .... Oldcastle ....

Which two journeys are the same length?

55–56 .... Newton .... to .... Northbury ....

57–58 .... Blackford .... to .... Canfield ....

59–60 Which is farther from Newton; Highville or Blackford?

.... Blackford ....

61–62 Which two places are half as far apart as Newton and Oldcastle?

.... Blackford .... and .... Northbury ....

[63–69]
In each of these lists underline the thing which does not fit in with all the others.

63	snake	frog	lizard	worm	<u>hedgehog</u>	toad	salamander
64	5	11	13	<u>18</u>	21	27	29
65	abc	cba	bca	<u>acbd</u>	cbd	dbc	acb
66	trawler	liner	yacht	<u>frigate</u>	tanker	tug	
67	pink	red	crimson	vermilion	<u>blue</u>	scarlet	
68	pink	daisy	dahlia	petunia	violet	viola	<u>violin</u>
69	saw	wrench	<u>screw</u>	chisel	plane	hammer	screwdriver

[70–74]
Underline the word in brackets which most correctly completes the sentence.

70 A car always has (a driver, fog lamps, <u>a fuel tank</u>, good brakes).
71 A house always has (a fire, three bedrooms, a bathroom, an occupier, <u>doors</u>).
72 A fish always has (a long tail, <u>fins</u>, a mate, big eyes).
73 Tape recorders always have (earphones, batteries, an on/off switch, <u>an electric motor</u>).
74 A train always has (a driver, passengers, wheels, seats, <u>a track</u>).

[75–84]
The typesetter has made a number of mistakes in the next paragraph. Can you sort them out?
Show me the person who does not want to be a catpain once in his life! You can rent a boat for a day, or a lehow week, and discover creste shecabe and beautiful coves all by sourfely. But be careful! When you leave the sheltered part of the dalnis you can suddenly run into high winds and rotsmy asse. Every year, harbour police recover boats which had to take regefu in a cove or which are just werdeck at sea.

75 <u>captain</u>   76 <u>whole</u>   77 <u>secret</u>   78 <u>beaches</u>   79 <u>yourself</u>
80 <u>island</u>   81 <u>stormy</u>   82 <u>seas</u>   83 <u>refuge</u>   84 <u>wrecked</u>

[85–98]
Here are some clues to a simple code based on one of the early codes used by spies many years ago.
3–1–20 = cat   4–15–7 = dog   2–1–4 = bad   1–14–25 = any
26–15–4–9–1–3 = zodiac
Complete the following message in code:

Bad	dogs	bark	all	the	time
2–1–4	4–15–7–19	2–1–18–11	1–12–12	20–8–5	20–9–13–5

Decode the following message:

23–5   6–9–14–4   20–8–9–19   17–21–5–19–20–9–15–14
 We   find   this   question

13–21–3–8
 much

20–15–15   8–1–18–4   16–12–5–1–19–5   19–5–14–4
 too   hard   Please   send

8–5–12–16
 help

[99–100]

99 Twice **r** is three times **s** and half of **s** is 8. What is **r**? ___24___

100 What is a quarter of 8 × 239 divided by 2? ___239___

PAPER 4

1–2 Cross out the third and seventh words in this sentence:
The third ~~engineer~~ died at sea ~~on~~ the seventh day after leaving port.

[3–4]
A 2p coin weighs the same as two 1p coins.

3 Which is worth more, 10 kg of pennies or 10 kg of 2p coins?

They are the same.

4 If a bag of 2p coins was worth £3, how much would a bag of 1p coins of the same weight be worth? £3

[5–6]
Cross out one word in this set which does not fit with all the others, and put a ring round the word which includes the remaining six.
Ireland (Island) Iceland Jersey Malta Cyprus Australia ~~Spain~~

7–9 Sort out these words and put related words together on the same line.
first end beginning finish start last

first and last usually go together
beginning and end usually go together
start and finish usually go together

[10–14]
Cross out the word that is closest in meaning to the opposite of the first word in each line:

10	slowly	run	walk	hurry	~~swiftly~~	lazily
11	fall	~~rise~~	raise	up	down	climb
12	expand	extract	lessen	lesson	~~contract~~	enlarge
13	swim	float	glide	dive	~~sink~~	drown
14	hate	like	lose	~~love~~	live	fear

[15–22]
Rearrange these sentences to make sense, and say whether they are true or false.

True or False

15–16 happy selfish is rarely a person

A selfish person is rarely happy .... True

17–18 in the dark can see cats

Cats can see in the dark .... True

19–20 pound a pennies hundred make two

Two hundred pennies make a pound... ....False...........

21–22 walking a bicycle than slower is riding

Walking is slower than riding a bicycle.............................. ....True...........

[23–24]
Cross out words to make these sentences sensible:

23 ~~In summer~~ I wear gloves ~~on my feet~~ to keep my hands warm.

24 At sixty km an hour a car will cover ~~twenty~~ four km in four minutes.

[25–29]
In each of these sets underline the correct answer in the brackets:

25 **nose** is to **smell** as **ear** is to (listen, hearing, <u>hear</u>, sound, noise)
26 **face** is to **mouth** as **house** is to (window, room, roof, stairs, <u>door</u>)
27 **face** is to **eyes** as **house** is to (<u>window</u>, room, roof, stairs, door)
28 **bird** is to **feathers** as **fish** is to (sea, <u>scales</u>, weight, fin, nest)
29 **often** is to **always** as **seldom** is to (sometimes, usually, occasionally, <u>never</u>)

[30–34]
In this set of words, ring the word that includes most of the others and cross out the words that do not fit.

~~beef~~   beet   peas   ~~dinner~~   (**vegetables**)   beans

~~apples~~   potatoes   turnips   cabbage   ~~currants~~

[35–39]
Read the passage and then underline the four words in the list which best describe the day.

I had been trapped in the house for over a week by the stormy weather, but now the sun was shining brightly so I took a walk in the country. The sky was blue and the birds sang in the trees. The air was warm for the first time for many months and I could see the newly formed buds on the trees and hedges.

hot   summer   cold   wintry   <u>bright</u>   <u>sunny</u>

wet   windy   fine   <u>spring</u>   May   autumn

[40–49]
In a school table-tennis competition the players are: Andrew, Emily, Daniel, Charles, Sarah, Kelly, Tom and William.

Round 1	Round 2	Round 3	Winner
Andrew			
Emily	Emily		
Daniel		Emily	
Charles	Daniel		
Sarah			Kelly
Kelly	Kelly		
Tom		Kelly	
William	Tom		

This is the table of their match. Complete the table with the following results.
Daniel who beat Charles lost to Emily.
Andrew was beaten by Emily who also beat Daniel.
Sarah lost to Kelly who beat Tom.
Tom beat William but lost to Kelly.
Emily who beat Daniel was beaten by Kelly.

[50–54]
In each of these sets of words, underline the word that is closest in meaning to the opposite of the word on the left:

50	**grief**	<u>joy</u>	sadness	melancholy	unhappy	pain
51	**wealth**	poor	rich	wealthy	<u>poverty</u>	miser
52	**tough**	hard	brittle	thick	<u>tender</u>	strong
53	**lend**	steal	<u>borrow</u>	repay	buy	give
54	**optimist**	hopeful	miserable	gloomy	<u>pessimist</u>	despairing

[55–60]
Fill in the next number in each of these series:

55	64	32	16	8	4			2
56	7	8	10	13	17	22		28
57	343	49	7	1				1/7
58	6	3	8	4	10	5	12	6
59	abc	bcd	cde	def	efg			fgh
60	az	by	cx	dw				ev

PAPER 4

[61–69]
Ian, Peter, Martin, Joanna and Maria are assessing their funds. They have £10 altogether. The girls have the same amount as the boys, but Joanna has £1 more than Maria.

61 How much have the boys altogether? £5

62 Maria has £2

Ian has as much as Peter and Martin together, and Peter has 50p more than Martin.

63 Who has most of all? .... Joanna

64 Who has least of all? .... Martin

65 How much more has Joanna than Martin? £2

66 Who has more, Ian or Maria? .... Ian

67–68 Maria and Ian together have exactly the same as Joanna and .... Peter

69 Martin and .... Joanna .... together have exactly the same as Ian and Peter.

[70–73]
In each of these sets, underline the correct answer in the brackets:

70 **man** is to **speak** as **dog** is to (howl, <u>bark</u>, cry, whimper)

71 **spring** is to **winter** as **childhood** is to (summer, autumn, <u>old age</u>, adulthood)

72 **rise** is to **fall** as **stop** is to (finish, end, <u>start</u>, begin)

73 **boat** is to **row** as **bicycle** is to (ride, <u>pedal</u>, steer, brake)

[74–78]
Here is a code. $a = 3, b = 2, c = 4, d = 6$

74 Divide **d** by **a** giving the answer as a number. 2

75 Multiply **b** by **a** giving the answer as a letter. .... d

76 What is the numerical answer to $(a + b) \times c$? 20

77 What number must be added to **a** to equal $c + d$? 7

78 What letter gives the answer to $\dfrac{a \times d}{b + c}$ .... a

[79–95]
A penfriend is trying to teach you a little of his native language. He starts off by giving you an example:
tana bona means **good boy** **maga bona** means **good dog**
freya bona means **good friend**
Bona comes three times and **good** comes three times so that **bona** must mean **good**. Then **tana** must mean **boy**, **maga** must mean **dog** and **freya** must mean **friend**.
He then writes sentences for you to try to work out the meaning of some more words.
Lado ingri dim = The girl read the book
Gan ingri sed = The mother read the letter
Lado madir la grad = The girl went to school
Gan madir la vild = The mother went to town
Lado madir la grad mit freya = The girl went to school with a friend
Gan madir la vild mit freya = The mother went to town with a friend

He then writes the sentence: **Lado y gan madir la vild mit freya y maga; lado y freya madir la grad.**

[79–94]
Write the sentence in English   *The girl and mother went to town with a friend and a dog; the girl and a friend went to school.*

95 Can you guess what **y** means?   *and*

96–97 Sheila's aunt is Mrs. Entwhistle, who has a daughter Jennie. What relation is Sheila's brother to Jennie's mother?   *Nephew*

[98–100]
These questions are to test whether you can follow instructions.

98 Turn back to question 52 in this paper. What is the third letter of the word in the third column?   *i*

99 Refer to questions 35–39 of this paper. What is the fourth word on the fourth line of the passage?   *months*

100 Turn to question 14 of this paper. How many four-letter words are there ending in **e**?   *5*

PAPER 5

[1–4]

1. What is the middle letter in this sentence?

   The continent of America is huge ......**f**......

2. A word is missing from this line. Put a cross where you think it should be and the word in the space provided.

   The stranger**✗**his way in the forest. ....**lost**..............

3. My birthday is on New Year's Day. David is 7 days older than I am.

   When is his birthday? ......**Christmas Day (25th December)**......

4. One number in this set does not fit. Put a ring around it.

   4 6 **(9)** 12 14 16

[5–7]
Add two further numbers to each of these series:

5. 3   6   9   12   15   ......**18**......   ......**21**......
6. 3   7   12   18   25   ......**33**......   ......**42**......
7. 46   35   25   16   ......**8**......   ......**1**......

[8–12]
Complete these lines by underlining the correct word in the brackets:

8. **uncle** is to **aunt** as **nephew** is to (cousin, <u>niece</u>, daughter, son)

9. **tree** is to **root** as **house** is to (roof, walls, leaves, rooms, <u>foundations</u>)

10. **same** is to **similar** as **rarely** is to (often, never, <u>seldom</u>, sometimes)

11. **deaf** is to **dumb** as **hearing** is to (seeing, <u>speaking</u>, words, noise, feeling)

12. **wood** is to **trees** as **town** is to (streets, <u>houses</u>, people, cinemas)

13. If I had another 30p I should have half as much as Lucy who needs 40p more to buy a ball costing £1.80. How much have I got? ......**40p**......

[14–18]
Fill in the missing signs to complete these sums.

14. 9 ..**+**.. 7 ..**−**.. 4 = 12

15. 18 ..**−**.. 9 ..**+**.. 5 = 14

16. 4 ..**×**.. 5 ..**×**.. 3 = 60

17. 36 ..**÷**.. 9 ..**×**.. 4 = 16

18. $\dfrac{17 \;\mathbf{+}\; 3 \;\mathbf{+}\; 8 = 4}{7}$

19–20 Cross out the three words that do not fit in with the rest of this set and ring the word which involves all the rest.

thimble   needle   ~~dressmaker~~   tape   thread   silk   scissors   buttons   (needlework)   ~~shoes~~   ~~socks~~

[21–26]
Here is a code. The five groups of figures stand for five words.
The figures are: 7534   1537   6557   4537   6536
and they stand for: rear   deal   lead   reel   meal
but not necessarily in that order. Which words do the following numbers stand for?

21 7534 = ...lead........   **22** 6557 = ...reel........
23 4537 = ...deal........   **24** 1537 = ...meal........
Give the numbers for:
25 leader = ...753456........   **26** lamed = ...73154........

[27–31]
Here are some anagrams or mixed up words.

27 **Noil** is a large wild animal. Write the proper name.   ....lion........

28 **Graone** is a common fruit. Write the last letter of the proper word.
........e........

29 **Arigut** is a musical instrument. Write the first letter of the proper word.
........g........

30 **Nosmi** is a boy's name. Write the first and last letters of his name.
........s, n........

31 **Sinosuch** are soft furnishings. Write the proper word.   ....cushions........

[32–37]
Complete the table:

	b	s	t
Fruit	banana	strawberry	tomato
Fish	bass/bream	shark	turbot
Vegetable	bean	spinach	turnip

[38–47]
Here are the names of some children in Classes 4, 5 and 6.

Class 6	Class 5	Class 4
David Strathmore	Julie Morgan	Maria
William Davis	Timothy Ames	Mary
Sarah Ames	Ann Strathmore	Brian
Joanne Morgan	Ian Davis	Peter
Mark Nichols	Helen Marchant	Karen

Can you find the surnames of the Class 4 children?
Here are some clues:
Maria has a brother in Class 6 and a sister in Class 5.
Mary has a brother in Class 5 and another in Class 6.
Brian has a sister in Class 6 and a brother in Class 5.
Peter has only one brother. He is in Class 6.
Karen has a sister in Class 6 and a sister in Class 5.

Maria ....*Strathmore*.... Mary ....*Davis*.... Brian ....*Ames*....

Peter ....*Nichols*.... Karen ....*Morgan*....

[48–54]
In each of the following sets, underline the two things that are alike and different from the rest:

48 winter   <u>Christmas</u>   summer   spring   <u>Easter</u>   autumn
49 police officer postman   soldier   <u>nurse</u>   <u>doctor</u>   sailor
50 shoes   tights   <u>necklace</u>   hat   <u>bracelet</u>   coat
51 horse   sheep   <u>zebra</u>   <u>camel</u>   cow   pig
52 needle   <u>thread</u>   <u>cotton</u>   tape   thimble   button
53 casserole dish frying pan   <u>basin</u>   kettle   saucepan   <u>jug</u>
54 George   Henry   <u>Mary</u>   Thomas   Richard   <u>Dianne</u>

[55–58]
Four boys, David, Jonathan, Gary and Ian, are keen sports players. David plays football, Jonathan plays cricket and tennis, Gary plays football and cricket and Ian plays cricket, tennis and rugby. On one particular afternoon they are all playing different games. Which game is each playing?

David ....*football*.... Jonathan ....*tennis*.... Gary ....*cricket*....

Ian ....*rugby*....

PAPER 5

[59–66]
Each of the following sets should show a definite order. Underline the items which should be first and last in each sequence.

59	rst	opq	<u>abc</u>	<u>wxy</u>	cde	qrs
60	959	919	839	<u>999</u>	<u>799</u>	879
61	August	June	April	September	<u>November</u>	<u>March</u>
62	88 cm	1 metre	<u>101 cm</u>	·86 metre	890 mm	
63	Jan 1987	<u>March 1987</u>	Nov 1986	<u>Nov 1985</u>	April 1986	
64	31p	33p	<u>£0.30</u>	£1.01	<u>£4.50</u>	99p
65	2 days	46 hrs	1.5 days	<u>54 hrs</u>	1.25 days	
66	¾	⅚	<u>½</u>	<u>⅘</u>	⅔	

[67–72]
The following names are those of well-known people. They are jumbled up. Can you sort them out?

67 **lien coinnkk** is a well known political figure ..... *Neil Kinnock*
68 **vidad rowge** plays cricket ..... *David Gower*
69 **yarg reelink** scores many goals ..... *Gary Lineker*
70 **hojn nelnno** was a famous musician ..... *John Lennon*
71 **theser tarzenn** is seen on television ..... *Esther Rantzen*
72 **richs tever** is often at Wimbledon ..... *Chris Evert*

[73–77]
In each of these sets, underline the word that is the opposite of the first word:

73	**receive**	take	lend	get	save	<u>give</u>	borrow
74	**over**	above	below	<u>under</u>	upon	higher	lower
75	**few**	crowd	collection	number	several	<u>many</u>	multitude
76	**famous**	eminent	<u>unknown</u>	ignorant	nobody		
77	**hide**	<u>reveal</u>	conceal	cover	discover	secret	

78 If tomorrow is Monday, what was the day before yesterday?
...... *Friday* ......

79 You are walking in the hills and walk 5 km north, then 4 km east, then 5 km south. How far are you now from where you started? Underline your answer.
5 km   2 km   3 km   <u>4 km</u>   10 km

PAPER 5

[80–90]
Mazes used to be a very popular feature of English country house gardens. One of the most famous examples is the maze at Hampton Court which was created in the reign of William III and is still extremely popular with tourists. Here is a plan of the maze.

80–84 Can you trace your way to the centre?

85–90 You have to write instructions which your friends can follow: At the entrance turn ....left........, walk straight on to the first junction, then turn ....right........; at the next junction turn ....right........; then walk on. At the next junction take the ....left........ turn. Walk to the next junction and take the ....left........ turn. Walk on and again take the ....left........ turn. Walk to the centre.

[91–100]
Here is a list of British monarchs who ruled between 1660 and 1901:

	Accession	Died	Age
Charles II	1660	1685	55
James II	1685	1688*	68
William III }	1689	1702	51
and Mary II }		1694	33
Anne	1702	1714	49
George I	1714	1727	67
George II	1727	1760	77
George III	1760	1820	81
George IV	1820	1830	67
William IV	1830	1837	71
Victoria	1837	1901	81

*James II was deposed in 1688, died 1701.

91 Which king had the longest reign? .... George III ....

92 Which monarch had the shortest reign? .... James II ....

93 Which queen was youngest on her accession? .... Victoria ....

94 Who reigned during the American War of Independence (1776)?
 .... George III ....

95 In whose reign did James Watt file the first patent for the steam engine (1769)?
 .... George III ....

96 Which monarch was oldest on accession to the throne? .... William IV ....

97 Which king founded the Greenwich Royal Observatory (1675)?
 .... Charles II ....

98 Which monarch reigned when the telephone was invented (1875)? .... Victoria ....

99 What was the average lifespan of the rulers after 1760? .... 75 yrs ....

100 Was there a time during the period covered by the chart when Britain had no monarch? If so, when? .... 1688–1689 ....

PAPER 6

1. In a churchyard stands a six-sided pillar. What is the largest number of sides you could see at the same time? ...... **3** ......

2. Put a circle inside a square unless 7 times 8 equals 56, in which case put a square inside a circle. ...... ⬡ ......

3–4 Draw a ring around the wrong answers.
50 pence are equal to: a half of £1   £0.50   (20 2p pieces)
5 10p pieces   (£0.05)   a tenth of £5

[5–9]
Cross out the words or parts of words which make these sentences silly:

5–7 Car~~rot~~ Ferries ~~march~~ across the Straits of Dover every day.

8 The whole group's ~~con~~science experiments were a failure.

9 One good turn~~ip~~ deserves another.

[10–14]
Complete these sentences by underlining the correct word in brackets:

10 **gas** is to **electricity** as **pipe** is to (tobacco, gas, <u>wire</u>, water, main)

11 **strong** is to **weak** as **push** is to (tug, <u>pull</u>, shove, resist)

12 **sum** is to **answer** as **problem** is to (work, <u>solve</u>, read, attempt)

13 **snooker** is to **football** as **indoor** is to (game, competition, prize, <u>outdoor</u>, fresh air)

14 **now** is to **time** as **here** is to (here, there, everywhere, <u>place</u>, when)

[15–24]
A grandmother wrote a shopping list for her grandchild to take to the greengrocer. She has used the right letters in the words but had spelled them all wrongly. Suppose you were the grandchild and had to find what she wanted. Here is the shopping list. Look at it and fill in the correct words.

5 kg of **spooteat**	= 5 kg of	...... potatoes ......
1 **ippepenal**	= 1	...... pineapple ......
2 **bacgbase**	= 2	...... cabbages ......
2 kg of **surbsles stroups**	= 2 kg of	...... brussels sprouts ......
12 **groanes**	= 12	...... oranges ......

PAPER 6

[25–27]
Jason is taller than Mary. Mary is shorter than Carl. Carl is taller than Rebecca. Underline your answer.

25 Is Rebecca taller than Jason?   Yes   No   <u>I cannot tell</u>

26 Is Mary taller than Carl?   Yes   <u>No</u>   I cannot tell

27 Is Carl taller than Jason?   Yes   No   <u>I cannot tell</u>

[28–32]

| C | L | O | I | S | T | E | R |

Put a letter in each square so that:
Each of the letters **C, L** and **I** is nearer to **O** than to **T**
Each of the letters **R, E** and **S** is nearer to **T** than to **O**
C, L, E, R are not between **O** and **T**
E is nearer to **T** than **R** is
C is at one end

[33–39]
In the drawing, three circles overlap, and there are numbers in the circles and in the overlapping parts.

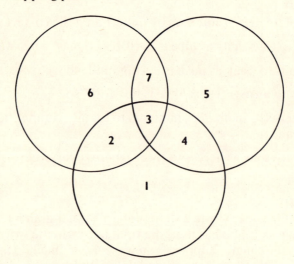

What are the numbers that are in one circle only? ....<u>1, 5, 6</u>........

Which numbers are in two circles only? ....<u>2, 4, 7</u>........

Which numbers are in three circles? ....<u>3</u>........

[40–41]
Find the correct word to complete the following:

40 **clock** is to **time** as **speedometer** is to ....<u>speed</u>........

41 **clock** is to **time** as **thermometer** is to ....<u>temperature</u>........

PAPER 6

[42–45]
Ring the words in this set that do not fit in with the rest and cross out the word whose meaning includes all the others.

desk   book   pencils   ~~school~~   chalk   bookcase   (ladder)
(smoke)   (mouse)   cupboard   easel   cloakroom   playground

[46–50]

A ————————————————————————— B
       12   24   36   48 km

A and B are two towns 48 km apart. A man starts to walk from A to B at 1000 hours, walking at 6 km per hour. At the same time a cyclist starts to ride from B to A at 18 km per hour. When and where will they meet?

They will meet at .....1200..... hours, ...12..... km from A.

51 Three times **a** = 4 times **b** and a half of **b** = 6. What is **a**?

.....16.....

[52–56]
Here are ten words that can be divided into five related pairs:
banana   wolf   well   doctor   skin
orange   water   pips   fur   sickness

Fill in the pairs:

52 .....banana..... and .....skin.....
53 .....wolf..... and .....fur.....
54 .....orange..... and .....pips.....
55 .....water..... and .....well.....
56 .....doctor..... and .....sickness.....

[57–61]
Underline the word in each set which is the opposite of the first word:

57 **seldom**   <u>often</u>   always   never   usually   occasionally
58 **tired**   fatigued   happy   lazy   <u>energetic</u>   sleepy
59 **wet**   showery   rainy   damp   sunny   <u>dry</u>
60 **innocent**   ignorant   clean   unhappy   wicked   <u>guilty</u>
61 **hurry**   walk   run   <u>loiter</u>   lazy   sit

62 What letter occurs only once in **different** and twice in **ordinary**? .....r.....

63 What letters in the word **entrance** appear as often as the last but one letter of the alphabet appears in **yesterday**? .....e, n.....

PAPER 6

[64–72]
You are designing a simple pattern, and have painted the top three squares blue, the middle three squares white and the bottom three red. You then paint them over, but this time the left-hand column of squares (**A, D, G**) are painted red, the middle column blue and the right-hand column white. The paints mix so that for example, a square that had a coat of red and then of white comes out pink, and one that had blue and then white comes out pale blue.

Which square comes out:

white? ......F......   blue? ......B......   red? ......G......

pale blue? C and E   pink? D and I   purple? A and H

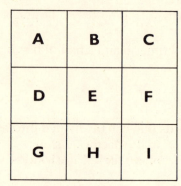

[73–82]
Fill in the missing words in the following passage from the list below.

Anyone who wishes to study mammals must know ......when...... and where to find them, and learn something about their habits. Most ......mammals...... are very timid and have such keen ......hearing...... and sense of ......smell...... that they will ......quickly...... be aware that you are nearby. Learn first to keep very ......still...... and to move ......quietly...... through leaves and bushes. Train yourself to ......listen...... for the smallest sounds which may be the only ......clue...... that there is an animal nearby. Never make quick or sudden ......movements.......

listen   movements   when   mammals   clue   quietly   still
hearing   quickly   smell

[83–84]
Underline the correct word in the brackets:

83 **cyclist** is to **ride** as **pedestrian** is to (run, walk, hitch-hike, travel)

84 **real** is to **unreal** as **knowledge** is to (doubt, think, imagination, ignorance)

[85–100]
Imagine that you are a person called Simon David Hall. He was born to Sheila and John Hall on 29th February, 1976. John, who is a toolmaker, was then twenty-eight and Sheila, who had been working as a nurse, was twenty-five. Sheila had a further son two years later and only returned to her old occupation when the younger child was eight. Simon went to the local junior school when he was seven and apart from short periods of illness has attended regularly. He is a handsome boy, tall with fair hair, though he is rather short-sighted. He wears glasses somewhat reluctantly because they interfere with his running and jumping and other sports. He is quite clever at maths and is old enough to progress to the secondary school. He is applying to attend a new school which especially encourages children who are very keen on maths and science and also has very good sports facilities.

Fill in this application form as if you were Simon, and the date was 20th July 1988.

PART I
TO BE FILLED IN BY ALL APPLICANTS

85 Your full name (Surname first)   Hall, Simon David
86 Full name of father   John Hall
87 Occupation of father   Toolmaker
88 Age of father   40
89 Full name of mother   Sheila Hall
90 Occupation of mother   Nurse
91 Age of mother   37
92 How many brothers or sisters do you have?   One brother
93 State your date of birth   29/2/1976
94 How many years have you attended your present school?   Five
95 Do you normally enjoy good health?   Yes
96 Do you have good sight (with glasses if normally worn)?   Yes
97 Do you suffer from any disability or nervous disorder?   No
98–99 Give your main reasons for wishing to attend this school.   I am good at maths which I enjoy. I am very keen on sports especially running and jumping.

DECLARATION
I apply to be accepted for St. Edmond's School in the September Term 1988. I declare that the above facts about me are true.

100 Signature of applicant   *S.D. Hall*   Date   20th July 1988

PAPER 7

a b c d e f g h i j k l m n o p q r s t u v w x y z

[1–3]

1. How many letters are there in the alphabet before **o**? ......14......

2. If you have as many pounds as there are letters in the alphabet after the letter **g**, how much more would you need to buy a personal cassette player costing £22? ......£3......

3. Which is the letter that comes next in the alphabet to the letter that first appears three times in this sentence? ......i......

4. Cross out all the odd numbers less than 9 in the following set:
   ~~3~~ 4 6 ~~7~~ 9 11 16 17 19 21

[5–11]
Complete the following proverbs:

5–6 A ......bird...... in the hand is worth two in the ......bush......

7–8 A watched ......pot...... never ......boils......

9 ......Empty...... vessels make most noise

10–11 Many ......hands...... make light ......work......

[12–14]
Underline the word that means the opposite of the first word in each set:

12 **strong**   weakness   feeble   week   rotten   <u>weak</u>

13 **humble**   rich   wealthy   powerful   <u>proud</u>   modest

14 **wide**   <u>narrow</u>   broad   expanse   near   deep

[15–16]
I have three coins. Coin **Z** is worth $\frac{1}{10}$ of Coin **Y** which has five times the value of Coin **X**. Coin **X** is $\frac{1}{10}$ of £1.

15 What value is Coin **Z**? ......5p......

16 What is the value of Coin **X** + Coin **Y**? ......60p......

17–18 Underline the sums which are correct:

<u>7 × 8 = 56</u>   8 × 7 = 63   <u>63 ÷ 9 = 7</u>   63 − 63 = 1   63 × 0 = 63

19–20 Share out 5 oranges among three children so that each has an odd number of oranges. ......One has 3, the others 1 each......

21 John is taller than any of his brothers, James, William or Peter. Peter is taller than James, but shorter than William. Who is the shortest? ...James...

22–23 Is this sentence correct? ......No...... If not, cross out one letter to make it right.
The sunrise caused a rosy glow over the w̸eastern sky.

24 I walk 10 metres to the west, 10 metres to the north and 10 metres to the south. How far am I from where I started? Underline the correct answer.
20 metres   60 metres   <u>10 metres</u>   at the exact point I started from

[25–27]
Complete the following by underlining the right words in brackets.

25 **true** is to **untrue** as **fact** is to (imagination, fancy, <u>fiction</u>, account)

26 **fair** is to **unfair** as **straight** is to (upright, wrong, doubtful, <u>crooked</u>)

27 **fair** is to **dark** as **empty** is to (enough, light, <u>full</u>, heavy)

[28–39]
In the following passage one word has been missed out of each line. Mark with a cross (x) where each missing word should be and supply the word at the end of each line.

28–29   In the winter the(x) often becomes stormy and   weather

30–31   cold, the wind(x) around the chimney pots,   whistles

32–33   and the(x) come rustling down from the trees   leaves

34–35   leaving them gaunt and(x) The heavy rains   bare

36–37   convert the streams(x) swollen torrents which   into

38–39   (x) their banks and flood the countryside.   burst/break/overflow

[40–44]
We have made nine lanterns for Halloween. They are made out of jam jars which have been painted and candles are put inside.
Jane, Alison and Anne have large lanterns.
David, Ian and Simon have lanterns made from medium-sized jars and Sian, Rosemary and Patrick have small lanterns.
Sian, Ian and Anne have painted their jars green.
Jane, David and Rosemary have coloured their lanterns red.
The other children have made their lanterns yellow.

Who has:

40 a large red lantern? Jane   41 a small green lantern? Sian

42 a large yellow lantern? Alison   43 a small red lantern? Rosemary

44 a medium yellow lantern? Simon

[45–46]
The list shows how far some towns are from Newtown:
Highchurch 15 km   Middleton 30 km   Farville 45 km   Tarton 20 km
Highton 10 km
A man cycled from Newtown to one of these towns at 15 km per hour. He left his bicycle to be repaired and walked back at 5 km per hour. The whole journey took him 4 hours 20 minutes including 20 minutes at the cycle repair shop. Which town did he visit? Highchurch

[47–54]
The numbers represent a code for the words above, but not in the given order:

acts   care   cats   scarf   star
5314   3514   45362   4136   5367

47 5314 = *cats*   48 3514 = *acts*   49 4136 = *star*

50 45362 = *scarf*   51 5367 = *care*

What number code would stand for these words?

52 crate = *56317*   53 tests = *17414*   54 treats = *167314*

[55–59]
Underline the correct word in brackets:

55 **wet** is to **damp** as **wind** is to (hurricane, gale, <u>breeze</u>, storm)

56 **lion** is to **cow** as **wild** is to (docile, friendly, tame, fierce, <u>domestic</u>)

57 **two** is to **four** as **four** is to (ten, fifteen, <u>eight</u>, twelve)

58 **three** is to **nine** as **nine** is to (eighteen, thirty-six, <u>twenty-seven</u>, twenty-four, forty-five)

59 **four** is to **eight** as **seven** is to (<u>fourteen</u>, 14, 21, 12)

[60–63]
Fill in the missing signs to complete these sums:

60 $19 + 3 \; \underline{-} \; 7 = 15$ 61 $12p + 6p \; \underline{-} \; 7p = 11p$

62 $(27 \; \underline{\div} \; 3) \times 2 = 18$ 63 $17 \; \underline{+} \; 13 \; \underline{-} \; 15 = 15$

64 If **x** = 3 times **a** and **a** = 3 times **b** and **b** = 3, what is **x**? *27*

65 My father is 3 times as old as I am. I am 9. How many times older than I, was my father 3 years ago? *4 times*

66 Underline the words in the set which are the same as another if spelled backwards:

cats acts arts <u>star</u> scar arcs <u>rats</u>

[67–75]
There are eight boys in a tug-of-war team. The captain of the team is John Williams; first name — John, surname — Williams. His initials are therefore J.W. Other surnames in the team are Jones, Smith, Walker, Robinson and Davies. Other first names are Gary, Richard, James, Hugh, Steve and Harry.
Two boys have surnames and first names beginning with the same letter. Two others have the same first name, Gary.
Hugh is the brother of the captain.
There are twins in the team, one with the same initials as the captain, the other with the same initials as the captain's brother. What are the boys' full names?

67	John	Williams	68	Hugh	Williams
69	Harry	Walker	70	Gary	Jones
71	Gary	Davies	72	Richard	Robinson
73	Steve	Smith	74–75	James Walker	

[76–87]
I have looked through the television guides for the week ahead and made a note of the programmes I particularly want to record. They are:

A Sunday   2.30 pm – 4.35 pm A musical film
B Monday   8.10 pm – 9.00 pm A science magazine programme
C Tuesday   7.00 pm – 7.30 pm A pop music programme
D Wednesday   7.30 pm – 9.15 pm International football
E Thursday   9.35 pm – 10.50 pm A play
F Saturday   11.30 am – 12.05 pm A short sci-fi feature

How long does each of the programmes last in minutes?

76 A 125   77 B 50   78 C 30   79 D 105
80 E 75   81 F 35

I have only two blank tapes, one for 180 minutes and the other for 240 minutes. How should I arrange my recording so that I can fit in all the programmes? Fill in the letters.

82–83 The three-hour tape should be used to record D and E
84–87 The four-hour tape should be used to record A, B, C, F

PAPER 7

88 Underline the word in this set which has no two letters the same:

   peaceful   sometimes   <u>friendly</u>   doubtful   backwards

89 If 7th March is a Wednesday, what is the third letter of the day of the week which falls on 17th March? ....t.............

90 Which letters in the word **frequent** come between **r** and **u** in the alphabet? ....t.............

[91–95]
In each of the following lists, underline the words that mean either the same as or the opposite of the first word.

91 **difference**   unlike   dislike   <u>likeness</u>   <u>similarity</u>

92 **abode**   house   tent   hut   <u>dwelling</u>

93 **loiter**   run   late   <u>hurry</u>   fast   travel

94 **calm**   friendly   ferocious   <u>turbulent</u>   <u>peaceful</u>   quiet

95 **reason**   answer   question   <u>argue</u>   consider

[96–100]
Can you sort out the mixed up words in the following passage?

96 Have you ever made a preap aeroplane or a paper   ....paper.............

97 boat? Ginkam objects from folded paper is one of   ....making.............

98 the oldest forms of lingmolde. The Japanese were   ....modelling.............

99 the veinronts of the art. They did not know how to   ....inventors.............

100 make paper aeroplanes but made wonderful nodgras and birds.

   ....dragons.............

PAPER 8

a b c d e f g h i j k l m n o p q r s t u v w x y z

1. The 1st, 12th, 16th, 8th, 1st, 2nd, 5th and 20th letters in the alphabet together form a word. What is it? .... *alphabet* ....

2. Counting **a** = 1, **b** = 2, **c** = 3, etc., what is the sum of the numbers standing for the word **horse**? .... *65* ....

3. Cross out a part of a word to make this sentence sensible:
   He grew his op~~i~~nions in his garden.

4. Which letter occurs most frequently in this sentence?
   I love fragrant flowers and fruit. .... *r* ....

5–6. Put a ring round the sums with incorrect answers:
   (7 + 3 = 21)   (21 = 7 + 3)   21 = 7 × 3   21⁄3 = 7

7. Who was the father of the son of William Shakespeare?
   .... *William Shakespeare* ....

8. In this sentence, two words are in the wrong place. Underline them.
   The widow <u>through</u> the ball <u>threw</u> the window.

9–10. One word is missing from this sentence. Mark its place with a cross and write it in at the end of the line.
   This book is different ✗ the one I gave you. .... *from* ....

[11–20]
Cross out the word in each of these sets which does not fit in with the others and ring the word which includes the rest:

11–12 (people)   miners   typists   sailors   women   ~~dogs~~   politicians
13–14 Dover   Hull   Harwich   London   ~~Leeds~~   (port)   Southampton
15–16 (European)   Swede   Swiss   Pole   Finn   Spaniard   ~~American~~
17–18 runner   jumper   swimmer   (athlete)   harrier   ~~snooker player~~
19–20 crocodile   alligator   lizard   snake   ~~otter~~   (reptile)

[21–25]
Complete these sets by underlining the correct word in the brackets:

21. **Friday** is to **Thursday** as **Monday** is to (Tuesday, Wednesday, <u>Sunday</u>, Friday, Saturday)

22. **strong** is to **weak** as **strengthen** is to (encourage, defeat, <u>weaken</u>, develop)

23. **England** is to **Surrey** as **country** is to (place, town, <u>county</u>, seaport, city)

24. **56** is to **28** as **98** is to (69, 196, 84, <u>49</u>)

25. **37** is to **51** as **51** is to (63, <u>65</u>, 71, 37)

[26–28]
Complete these series by adding the next two numbers:

26 1 5 9 13 17 21 ....25.... ....29....
27 20 15 10 5 ....0.... ....−5....
28 20 15 11 8 ....6.... ....5....

[29–38]
One word in each line in the following passage is spelled incorrectly. Put the corrected word in the space at the end of the line.

29 John went for a walk in the diefls .... fields ....
30 on a lovely fine day in ustuga, when .... August ....
31 the dribs were singing merrily in .... birds ....
32 the steer. As he walked he could see .... trees ....
33 the cows in the domewas swishing .... meadows ....
34 their itals as hard as they could to .... tails ....
35 vired away the flies which troubled .... drive ....
36 them. The path lead by the irrev and .... river ....
37 he idotnec that many of the cows .... noticed ....
38 were daginnst in the water to keep cool. .... standing ....

[39–48]
In each of the sets there are two correct answers. Underline both.

39–40 Lead is a (stone, vegetable, <u>mineral</u>, poker, <u>metal</u>)
41–42 Grass is (blue, <u>a plant</u>, dry, wet, <u>green</u>, long)
43–44 A lion is (black, tame, young, old, <u>wild</u>, <u>strong</u>)
45–46 Stockholm is in (France, Denmark, <u>Europe</u>, Russia, <u>Sweden</u>, Norway)
47–48 New York is a (<u>port</u>, capital, country, <u>city</u>, village)

[49–52]
Underline the correct answer in the brackets:

49 **question** is to **answer** as **problem** is to (solve, detective, <u>solution</u>, teacher)
50 **failure** is to (prize, disappointment, <u>success</u>, difficulty) as **right** is to **wrong**
51 **1** is to **10** as **100** is to (<u>1000</u>, 10,000, 100, 500, 10)
52 **one** is to **tenth** as **pound** is to (50p, 2p, <u>10p</u>, 1p)

[53–62]
Here is a town plan. Follow the directions carefully and add to the map the things that you are asked.
Starting from **A** travelling south, I crossed the river bridge which we will call **B1** and then passed the church (**C**) on my left. On the other side of the street and facing the church was the museum (**M**). After passing these I immediately came to the crossroads where I turned left, and passing the hotel (**H**) on my right I went under the railway bridge (**B2**). Turning around I went back to the crossroads and turning left passed the school (**S**) on my right just before I came to the next railway bridge (**B3**). I was just getting to this bridge when I remembered that I had to post a letter, so I turned around and went back to the crossroads again. Here I turned left and a short distance up the street found the post office (**PO**) on my right.

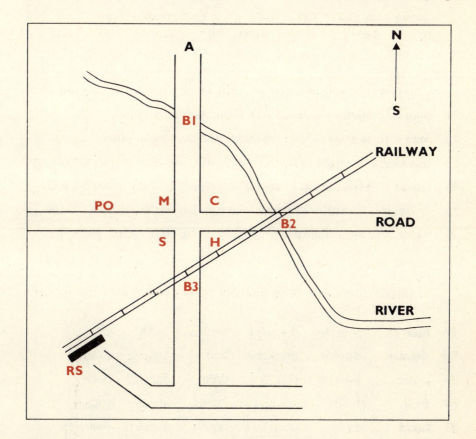

Place **B1, B2, B3, C, M, H, PO, S** and the railway station which you can mark **RS**.
Give the shortest directions you can to a person at the Post Office wishing to go to the railway station. Turn left, turn right at the crossroads, then take the first turning to the right.

[63–65]
Cross out what you need to make the following statements sensible:

63 One fifth of three pounds and twenty ~~five~~ pence is sixty-four pence.

64 Travelling at thirty kilometres per hour a car will cover seventy ~~two~~ kilometres in a hundred and forty minutes.

65 If I am walking at four kilometres per hour I am going faster ~~slower~~ than David who is covering a kilometre every twenty minutes.

[66–70]
Cross out the words that do not fit with the others and ring the word that includes the rest:

~~young~~ ~~careless~~ little ~~old~~ (size) small large
tall ~~heavy~~ stout short big thin

[71–76]
Complete the following by underlining the correct word in brackets:

71 **man** is to **monkey** as **hand** is to (hair, tail, claw, <u>paw</u>)

72 **man** is to **woman** as **fox** is to (hen, female, <u>vixen</u>, cub)

73 **morning** is to **night** as **birth** is to (youth, old age, childhood, <u>death</u>)

74 **friend** is to **friendship** as **enemy** is to (hostile, fight, <u>enmity</u>, war)

75 **summer** is to **winter** as **youth** is to (<u>age</u>, death, adulthood, father)

76 **water** is to **ice** as **liquid** is to (frozen, cold, <u>solid</u>, hard, glassy)

[77–82]
In each of these sets, underline the word which means the opposite of the first word.

77	**hide**	secrete	<u>discover</u>	confess	seek	safe
78	**sickness**	doctor	medicine	bed	<u>health</u>	disease
79	**work**	holiday	<u>rest</u>	dole	lazy	poor
80	**fresh**	fruity	delicious	lovely	nasty	<u>rotten</u>
81	**build**	erect	<u>destroy</u>	bomb	repair	damage
82	**eat**	food	meal	<u>fast</u>	drink	devour

[83–94]
Eight schoolfriends are keen members of a local sailing club. They are all good sailors and want to choose a crew of two to sail a boat in the County Junior Championships. The usual sailing partners are:
Sarah (30 kg)   and   Sophie (36 kg)
Neil (56 kg)   and   Yvonne (50 kg)
Jeremy (60 kg) and   James (40 kg)
Sian (54 kg)   and   Simon (34 kg)
Small sailing boats go faster in light winds with a light crew while in strong winds a heavy crew has an advantage. Therefore, Sarah and Sophie would expect to do well on calm days while Neil and Yvonne would do best when it was very windy.
In their selection trials they decided to compete in similar boats with crews chosen so that each boat carried a similar weight. Who were the four crews in the selection trials?

83–84   ....Sarah.... sailed with ....Jeremy....

85–86   ....Neil.... sailed with ....Simon....

87–88   ....Sian.... sailed with ....Sophie....

89–90   ....Yvonne.... sailed with ....James....

They all came so close that they decided to have two crews ready for the Championships, one to sail if the winds were very strong, and the other crew in case it was a calm day. Their chosen crews were:

91–92   Strong winds: ....Jeremy.... sailing with ....Neil....

93–94   Light winds: ....Sarah.... sailing with ....Simon....

[95–97]
Seven years ago I was 12 years old and my father was then three times as old as I was.

95   How old was he when I was born?   ....24....

96   How old will I be when my father is 60?   ....36....

97   In how many years time will my father's age be twice mine?
                                                   ....5....

98   If my watch shows the time as 0955 hours and I mistook the position of the two hands, what time would I think it was?   ....1050 hours....

[99–100]
Sort out these mixed up words:

99   **cutremops** are fun for playing games on   ....computers....

100   **grayplsound** are fun for playing games in ....playgrounds....

PAPER 9

1. Underline the sixth word in this sentence:
   This is the sixth time <u>she</u> has swum for the school.

2. Cross out part of a word to make this sentence sensible:
   He was often seen with~~out~~ his coat on, and that is why he was so hot.

[3–7]
In a grey cottage between two newly whitewashed ones, lived Sarah aged 9 with her parents and three younger brothers. In one of the whitewashed ones lived Mr. and Mrs. Nelson and their three children while the other was occupied by an old couple, Mr. and Mrs. Simes.

3. Which house had most people living in it? ..... Sarah's
4. How many houses were there? 3
5. How many people altogether lived in the houses? 13
6. How many grey houses were there? 1
7. How many children lived in the houses? 7

8–9. Cross out the unwanted word or part of a word in these sentences:
   The herd of elephants furiously charged the marauding lions ~~sixpence~~.
   The hill fort~~night~~ was regained by the army without a struggle.

[10–12]
Arrange these words putting similar things together:
nine   twentieth   tenth   twelve

10. nine and ..... twelve ..... go together
11–12. ..... tenth ..... and ..... twentieth ..... go together

[13–21]
Fill in the missing figures where the dots are in these two sums.

13–16
```
  7964
  6735
  6849
 -----
 21548
```

17–21
```
   7129
     27
  -----
  49903
  14258
 ------
 192483
```

22–23. Ring the two best answers:

I drink at least a pint of milk a day because:
(a) Milk is cheap   (b) I am thirsty
(c) (I like milk)   (d) (Milk is good for me)

[24–29]
Put a cross where a word is missing and supply the missing word.

24–25	In winter when the✗are wet and dark I	nights
26–27	do not go✗much but stay in the house	out
28–29	playing games and reading.✗	books

[30–42]
Cross out the words in brackets which would make these sentences wrong:

30–31 She (won, ~~one~~) (two, ~~to, too~~) prizes at the show.

32–33 He wondered (~~wear~~, where) the old (~~which~~, witch) had gone.

34–35 The (~~wether, whether~~, weather) has been poor and the (~~rein~~, rain, ~~reign~~) heavy this summer.

36–38 It was (plain, ~~plane~~) that they did not want him so he (~~staid~~, stayed) in and played with his (~~presence~~, presents).

39–42 He (~~lie~~, lay, ~~laid~~) (~~their~~, there) in (~~grate~~, great) (~~pane~~, pain).

[43–53]
In this passage one word on each line is mixed up. Put the correct word in the space.

43	Farmers enjoy the challenge of gramfin because	farming
44	although it is an dirtysun, it is one of the few	industry
45	that still fefor people a chance to pit their wits	offer
46	against the forces of Nature. Even with the leastt	latest
47	methods and every form of endrom farm machinery	modern
48	and chemical, a farmer can never be quite nictare	certain
49	when he sows a crop that the surlets will be what	results
50	he expects. There may be a sudden dofol, or constant	flood
51	rain during the harvest, new kinds of seaside of	disease
52	crops, or attacks by tissnec or other pests which	insects
53	have built up a resistance to milcache control.	chemical

PAPER 9

[54–63]
Look at the two columns of figures, and then follow the instructions:

987274	987772 .... O ....
984732	978742 ....
988364 .... L	982642 .... E ....
987472 .... A	984275 .... F ... x ....
981081 .... N .... x	928742 .... S ....
983764	987472 .... A ....

54 Put **L** for **largest** opposite the highest number.

55 Put **S** for **smallest** opposite the lowest number.

56–57 If you can find two numbers the same put **A** for **alike** opposite each of them.

58 One number can obviously be divided by 9; write **N** for **nine** opposite it.

59 Opposite the number containing the greatest number of odd digits write the letter **O** for **odd**.

60 Opposite the number containing the greatest number of even digits write **E** for **even**.

61 One number can be divided by 5; put **F** for **five** opposite it.

62–63 Two of the numbers cannot be divided by 2. Put a cross (**x**) opposite each of them.

[64–68]
Cross out the words which do not belong with the others and ring the word that includes all the rest:

honour   **goodness**   ~~place~~   ~~prize~~   **love**   **truth**   **faith**
(**quality**)   **benevolence**   **honesty**   ~~reward~~   ~~society~~   **beauty**

[69–72]
Complete the following by underlining the correct word in brackets:

69 **sail** is to **yacht** as **drive** is to (boat, sea, <u>car</u>, wheel)

70 **London** is to **England** as **capital** is to (labour, <u>country</u>, interest, county)

71 **known** is to **unknown** as **past** is to (history, present, forgotten, tell, <u>future</u>)

72 **truth** is to **lie** as **guide** is to (false, mistake, <u>mislead</u>, correct)

[73–77]
Atkins, Barnes, Chandler, Dawes and Edwards live in a terrace of five houses. Barnes lives two doors to the right of Atkins and next door to Dawes on the other side. Edwards lives next door to Atkins on his left.

73 Who lives on the extreme right of the terrace? ..... Dawes .....
74 Who lives on the extreme left? ..... Edwards .....
75 Who lives in the middle house? ..... Chandler .....
76–77 Who lives next door to Chandler? Atkins and Barnes

[78–82]
In each of the following sets, underline the word in brackets which is most like the three words outside the brackets:

78 house   bungalow   mansion   (kennel   sty   den   <u>palace</u>)
79 colt   calf   pup   (cow   dog   mare   veal   <u>cub</u>)
80 boot   shoe   slipper   (stocking   sock   <u>sandal</u>   scarf)
81 hat   cap   helmet   (hair   head   comb   <u>beret</u>)
82 chair   table   desk   (chimney   smoke   <u>cupboard</u>   chalk)

[83–87]
Anthony, Bruce, Charles, Darren and Edward are five boys. Edward is the lightest. Charles and Edward together are heavier than Anthony and Darren. Anthony and Bruce are together heavier than Bruce and Darren. Bruce is lighter than Anthony but heavier than Darren. Put them in order according to weight:

83 Heaviest ..... Charles .....   84 2nd ..... Anthony .....   85 3rd ..... Bruce .....
86 4th ..... Darren .....   87 5th ..... Edward .....

[88–91]
Underline the two things which are most alike but different from the rest:

88 <u>rind</u>   clang   bang   twang   peal   <u>peel</u>   blow
89 <u>solicitor</u>   doctor   teacher   vicar   <u>lawyer</u>
90 apple   <u>orange</u>   raspberry   tomato   <u>lemon</u>   plum   banana
91 <u>scooter</u>   bus   van   car   driver   train   <u>bicycle</u>

PAPER 9

[92–94]
Underline the word in brackets which best fits:

92 **always** is to **never** as **often** is to (sometimes, never, frequently, <u>seldom</u>)

93 **morning** is to **night** as **birth** is to (young, age, summer, <u>death</u>, winter)

94 **fifteen** is to **three** as **one** is to (a third, a fourth, <u>a fifth</u>, a sixth, a seventh)

[95–100]
The following are the instructions printed on a box of sticky labels. Unfortunately the printer had become confused and printed them in the wrong order. Put them in the right order by writing the correct number in the space after the instruction.

95 Stick the labels on the envelopes 6

96 Peel the labels from the backing paper 5

97 Pull a foot or so from the roll of labels 1

98 Feed the labels into the typewriter 2

99 Stand the carton behind the typewriter 3

100 Type the addresses on as many labels as you require 4

PAPER 10

1. Cross out every word in this sentence beginning with the letter **i**.
2. If 6 is less than 7 put **A** between **X** and **Y** unless 8 is less than 9, in which case put **O** between two **M**'s. ......M.O.M......
3. If an elephant is bigger than a mouse, put a square in a circle. If not, put a circle in a square. ......⊡......
4. The ages of two boys added together is 16. What will be the sum of their ages in ten years' time? ......36......
5. Four girls sit on a park bench. Helen sits at the right-hand end. Barbara sits to the right of Julie but to the left of Tina. Who is sitting on the left-hand end of the bench? ......Julie......
6. I am standing in the sun and facing south. My shadow is long on my left-hand side. What part of the day is it? ......Evening......
7. I go to school in the morning by bus. If I sit on the left side of the bus the sun is shining in on me. In what direction is the bus travelling? ......South......
8. If you were born in 1878, put a square in a circle. Otherwise, put a cross in a circle. ⊗

9–10. In the following set, one word describes most of the others. Underline it. Cross out the word that is not included by the underlined word:

Italy   France   Luxembourg   Spain   Greece   <u>Europe</u>   Norway   ~~Egypt~~

11–12. Number these in order of size, starting with the smallest:

county ......5......   district ......4......   town ......3......   village ......2......
hamlet ......1......   country ......6......   continent ......7......

[13–16]
Using this list of words, follow the instructions:

(through)   roof   ~~pavement~~   <u>smooth</u>   hedge   (foundation)

13. Put a ring round the word that has **o** as its middle letter.
14. Underline the word that means the opposite of **rough**.
15. Cross out the word that is associated with a street.
16. Put brackets round the word that contains the greatest number of vowels.

PAPER 10

[17–28]
These questions are about classification — grouping things which have common properties. Example: **elephant – lion   horse – rat**
Elephant and **lion** go together because they are animals that usually live outside the British Isles.
Horse and **rat** go together because they are animals that live in the British Isles.
We can also put them together in another way.
Elephant and **horse** go together because they do not normally eat meat, but they eat plants; they are herbivores.
Lion and **rat** go together because they eat flesh; they are carnivores.
Now arrange the following in groups because of some way in which they are alike:

cat   cow   squirrel   dog   sparrow   sheep   rabbit   robin   duck   pig   rat   pony

17–19   ......cat...... and ......dog...... and ......pony...... go together because they are pets

20–22   ......cow...... and ......sheep...... and ......pig...... go together

23–25   ......sparrow...... and ......robin...... and ......duck...... go together

26–28   ......rat...... and ......squirrel...... and ......rabbit...... go together

29   The following words contain some letters which are repeated. Underline the word which has most repeated letters:

possession   difficulty   committee   <u>accommodation</u>

30   Which letters occur twice only in **greatness** and once only in **friendship**?

......e and s......

31   Which letter occurs once in **greatness** and twice in **preserve**?   ......r......

[32–40]
Underline the word or figures in the brackets which fits best:

32   **today** is to **yesterday** as **tomorrow** is to (Monday, Tuesday, <u>today</u>, yesterday, some day)

33   **metre** is to **distance** as **hour** is to (day, length, <u>time</u>, year, week)

34   **metre** is to **kilometre** as **gram** is to (weight, tonne, milligram, <u>kilogram</u>, heavy)

35   **brush** is to **paint** as **pencil** is to (drawer, sentence, drawing, word, <u>draw</u>)

36   **pound** is to **penny** as **century** is to (day, month, <u>year</u>, hour)

37   **17** is to **34** as **19** is to (28, 36, <u>38</u>, 48, 57)

38   **26** is to **13** as **18** is to (36, 48, 32, <u>9</u>, 3, 12)

39   **19** is to **30** as **37** is to (43, <u>48</u>, 49, 51, 53)

40   **87** is to **64** as **46** is to (35, 27, <u>23</u>, 92, 69)

[41–46]
In each of the following sets, underline the word which has the opposite meaning to the first word:

41	concrete	wall	stone	indefinite	<u>abstract</u>	solid
42	sad	melancholy	loud	boisterous	<u>happy</u>	laughing
43	scarce	many	few	<u>plentiful</u>	luxuriant	lots
44	youth	old	man	child	adulthood	<u>age</u>
45	accidental	purpose	thought	desired	<u>deliberate</u>	chance
46	agree	argue	dispute	friendly	different	<u>differ</u>

[47–49]
Emma and Tom are cousins. Emma lives in Upper Haybury and Tom in Lower Haybury, which is 10 kilometres away by the main road. They agree to meet each other and start walking from their homes at 0900 hours one Saturday morning, following the main road. They are both good walkers and manage 5 kilometres an hour.

47 At what time will they meet? .... *1000 hours* ....

48 How far will they be from Upper Haybury when they meet?

.... *5 km* ....

49 Having had a good conversation they start back for home at 1200 hours, walking at the same speed. How far apart will they be at 1230 hours?

.... *5 km* ....

[50–54]
In each line there is one word which does not fit with the others. Underline it.

50	street	road	<u>shops</u>	highway	thoroughfare	avenue
51	Paris	London	Rome	Madrid	Lisbon	<u>Cape Town</u>
52	car	lorry	bus	<u>train</u>	motor-cycle	taxi
53	Nile	Thames	Clyde	Severn	<u>Everest</u>	Amazon
54	France	Germany	Austria	<u>Moscow</u>	Belgium	Holland

[55–58]

55–56 What relation to you is the only son of your father's father?

.... *Father* ....

57–58 What relation to Mr. Banks is the son of Mr. Banks' brother's wife?

.... *Nephew* ....

PAPER 10

[59–68]
In every line of the following passage one word is jumbled. Put the correctly spelled word in the space.

59	As we passed through the rood and entered the	door
60	dining room we noticed the grandfather lcokc	clock
61	on the side nearest the prefcaiel, where a	fireplace
62	rigroan fire blazed merrily and made little	roaring
63	lights shine in the slags ornaments on the	glass
64	breaddois, while on the opposite side of the	sideboard
65	room a great rirrom reflected the rosy glow.	mirror
66	The gold and black sutrinca which had been	curtains
67	drawn across the wodwin matched exactly the	window
68	thick percat which covered most of the room.	carpet

[69–76]
Mr. Hales was going to act in a play. He was being measured for his costume. The measurements were 61 cm, 165 cm, 43 cm, 13 cm, 71 cm and 112 cm. Which measurement did each figure refer to?

chest ..... 112 ..... cm   height ..... 165 ..... cm   neck ..... 43 ..... cm
wrist ..... 13 ..... cm   jacket length ..... 71 ..... cm   arm ..... 61 ..... cm
Was Mr. Hales a tall or a short man? ..... Short
Was Mr. Hales thin or fat? ..... Fat

77 I have six pairs of socks: two pairs of grey socks, two pairs of black ones, and two pairs of brown ones. They are all mixed up in a drawer. I go in the dark to get a pair of socks; how many single socks must I take to be sure of having a pair? ..... Four

[78–82]
Complete the following by underlining the correct word in the brackets:

78 **big** is to **biggest** as **good** is to (bad, <u>best</u>, better, greatest, excellent)
79 **Italy** is to **Europe** as **country** is to (state, county, <u>continent</u>, peninsular, nation)
80 **great** is to **greatness** as **graceful** is to (gracious, graciousness, dainty, <u>grace</u>, gracefully)
81 **car** is to **steering wheel** as **yacht** is to (sail, <u>tiller</u>, rudder, anchor, keel)
82 **hair** is to **comb** as **lawn** is to (hoe, lawnmower, <u>rake</u>, spade, fork)

[83–91]
There are nine school bags hanging on pegs in the school cloakroom. The bags on pegs 1, 4 and 6 are black. The bags on pegs 2, 5 and 8 are green. The other three bags are blue. The bags on pegs 1, 5 and 7 are small. The bags on pegs 2, 4 and 8 are large and the others are of medium size.

83 Alison has a small black bag. Which is her peg? ....1.......
84–85 Linda and Carla have large green bags. Which are their pegs?
.......2 and 8.......
86–87 Fiona and Cathy have medium blue bags. Which are their pegs?
.......3 and 9.......
88 Helen has a medium black bag. Which is her peg? ....6.......
89 Julia has a small blue bag. Which peg is Julia's? ....7.......
90 Jenny has a large black bag. Which peg does Jenny have?
.......4.......
91 Which bag is left on a peg after all these have been taken?
A small green bag

PAPER 10

[92–100]
Your big brother has asked you to do the last bit of his paper round for him as he doesn't have time to do it all before it is time for school. He has given you this street plan showing the houses that are left on the round and leaves the papers for you to deliver, at your house. Study the plan and decide on the quickest way to complete the paper round for him and get home for breakfast.

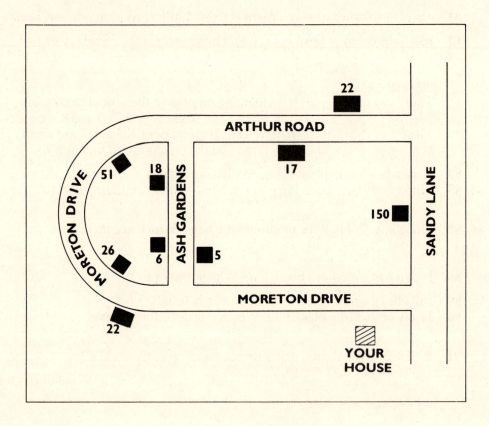

92	1st house	5 Ash Gardens
93	2nd house	6 Ash Gardens
94	3rd house	22 Moreton Drive
95	4th house	26 Moreton Drive
96	5th house	51 Moreton Drive
97	6th house	18 Ash Gardens
98	7th house	17 Arthur Road
99	8th house	22 Arthur Road
100	9th house	150 Sandy Lane

PAPER 11

[1–4]

1–2 Underline the word that has the greatest number of adjacent pairs of identical letters, and ring any words that have no letter occurring twice:

<u>committee</u>   relative   destination
accommodation   plentiful   (relation)

3–4 In this sentence put a ring around the middle letter of the middle word, and then see which vowel occurs most often in the sentence and write down the vowel and the number of times it occurs:

The song of the night(i)ngale has frequently been recorded. ..... e 9 .....

[5–9]
Five girls live in my street: Alice, Bronwen, Carla, Davina and Emily. Alice, Bronwen and Davina are tall; the others are short. Bronwen, Davina and Emily wear glasses. Alice and Carla do not like each other, but Alice is friendly with Bronwen and Emily, and Carla is friendly with Davina.

5–6 I noticed a short girl wearing glasses playing with a tall girl without glasses. Who were they? ..... Emily ..... and ..... Alice .....

7 A little later a tall girl with glasses joined them. Who was it?
..... Bronwen .....

8 I saw a short girl without glasses walk straight past Alice without speaking. Who was she? ..... Carla .....

9 This girl called at a house further down the street and was joined by a tall girl with glasses. Who was she? ..... Davina .....

[10–12]
Cross out any word or part of a word not wanted in these sentences:

10 I am not ~~know~~ going home to tea.

11 The man had corns on some of his ~~tom~~atoes.

12 The old man left all his money to his wi/ndow.

13 Complete the line with the correct word:

he is to **she** as **him** is to ..... her .....

14 Put the letter **A** between C and D if 7 is more than 8; if not put **D** between C and E. ..... CDE .....

15 Do exactly what you are told in this question:
How old are you? Write nothing but the answer to this question:

I am ..... X ..... years old. I live in ....
X = age of the person answering

PAPER 11

[16–18]
Pair the following words:

iron   steal   steel   take

16   iron and ....*steel*........ go together

17–18   ....*take*........ and ....*steal*........ go together

[19–26]
In each of the following sets of words, underline the word in brackets that goes best with the first three words and is different from the other words in brackets.

19   beans   beet   turnips   (meat   gravy   sauce   apples   <u>peas</u>)
20   table   chair   sofa   (ceiling   picture   <u>stool</u>   mirror)
21   elm   oak   ash   (hue   beach   acorn   grass   <u>beech</u>)
22   rake   fork   hoe   (crowbar   hammer   nail   plane   <u>spade</u>)
23   run   walk   swim   (talk   sit   think   watch   <u>jump</u>   see)
24   rotten   bad   wicked   (good   happy   sad   <u>evil</u>   coarse)
25   cat   dog   horse   (rat   mouse   sheep   badger   <u>pony</u>)
26   talk   argue   discuss   (think   smile   <u>shout</u>   weep   consider)

[27–33]
Mary Smith is the mother of Lisa Smith, so Lisa Smith must be the daughter of Mary Smith. Now do these:

27   Miranda Brown is the niece of John Brown, so John Brown is the ....*uncle*........ of Miranda Brown.

28   Nottingham is 80 km north-east of Birmingham, so Birmingham is 80 km ....*south-west*........ of Nottingham.

29–30   The park is 350 m north-west of the Town Hall, so the Town Hall must be ....*350 m*........ m ....*south-east*........ of the park.

31   Mr. Hill was my predecessor as headmaster, so I am Mr. Hill's ....*successor*........ as headmaster.

32   If William the Conqueror were my ancestor I would be a ....*descendant*........ of William the Conqueror.

33   If Queen Elizabeth II succeeded King George VI as monarch of the United Kingdom, George VI ....*preceded*........ Elizabeth II.

[34–44]
Here is a timetable of trains between London and Southampton:

London dep.	0910	1040	1230	1315	1515	1745	2110	2330
Southampton arr.	1120	1255	1435	1540	1705	1910	2310	0018

34–36 When does the fastest train of the day leave for Southampton? ....1745 hours..........

37–38 Which is the slowest train of the day? ....1315 hours..........

39–42 Between what times are there no trains travelling between London and Southampton? ......1910...... and ......2110...... ......0018...... and ......0910......

43–44 Suppose you stood on a bridge overlooking the line halfway between the two places from 1420 to 1440 hours. Which train would pass beneath you?

..........1315 hours..........

[45–52]
Here is a code where figures stand for letters. Work out the code, and then answer the questions.

The words are: mate seat treat great meat team
and the numbers: 3257 1257 1572 46257 76257 7251

Translate into code:

45 mate ......1572...... **46** seat ......3257...... **47** treat ......76257......
48 great ......46257...... **49** meat ......1257...... **50** team ......7251......

Decode:

51 65723 ......rates...... **52** 37567 ......start......

[53–56]
Two friends, Simon and Sheila, set out from the same place on their bicycles, heading for the same destination. They both ride at a steady speed, but at a place 4 km from where they started Simon passes Sheila. Underline the correct answer:

53–54 Simon must have been riding (<u>faster than</u>, at the same speed as, slower than) Sheila.

55–56 Simon must have started (before, <u>after</u>, at the same time as) Sheila.

[57–69]
In the following passage, a number of words have become jumbled through a typesetting error. Write the words, correctly spelled, at the end of the line.

57 Some people who watch vitelnoise or horror films will   television
58 think of the itsnicest as a strange being, inhabiting   scientist
59 a room filled with bubbling glassware and circleet   electric
60 sheflas; some may see him as a sinister figure intent   flashes
61 on committing some evil against dinkman, while others   mankind
62 think of him as a person who can find a cure for souries   serious
63 seaside or generally make life better for all of us.   disease
64 But these ideas are misleading. A scientist is a sprone   person
65 who has developed the skills to seek rensaws to problems
                                                                  answers
66 in a special way. A scientist may have a porkshow and   workshop
67 call it a barrytoola, but the important thing is not the   laboratory
68 shiny quenemtip in it but the methods by which he works.
                                                                  equipment
69 Although the text above refers frequently to the scientist as "him", are all scientists men? .... No ....

[70–74]
Underline the most suitable word in the brackets:
70 **foot** is to **hand** as **toe** is to (foot, <u>finger</u>, ankle, bone)
71 **mend** is to **repair** as **break** is to (<u>damage</u>, renew, improve, wear)
72 **forget** is to **remember** as **question** is to (ask, demand, inquire, <u>answer</u>, reveal)
73 **night** is to **day** as **acid** is to (corrosive, <u>alkali</u>, lemon, vinegar)
74 **bat** is to **ball** as **hammer** is to (screw, chisel, <u>nail</u>, finger)

PAPER 11

[75–79]

Thomas, Jason, Lucy and Harriet are friends and keen tennis players. They are all at school all day during the week. Thomas has trumpet lessons on Monday, Wednesday and Friday evenings. Jason has cricket practice in the evening on Monday and Tuesday, and plays matches on Saturday. Lucy has cello classes on Tuesday, Thursday and Saturday evenings. Harriet is free only on Monday, Tuesday and Saturday evenings. The school tennis courts are not open on Sunday mornings or evenings.

75 Which evening can Thomas and Jason play together?   *Thursday*

76 Which evenings can Jason and Lucy play together?

    Wednesday and *Friday*

77 When can Lucy and Harriet play together?

    Monday and *Sunday afternoon*

78 Which evenings can Thomas and Harriet play together?

    Tuesday and *Saturday*

79 When can they play a mixed doubles match?   *Sunday afternoon*

[80–84]

80 Underline the middle thing in order of size:

    pencil   matchstick   flagpole   beanstick   <u>cricket-stump</u>

81 Underline the smallest animal in this list:

    elephant   mouse   fly   rat   lion   horse   <u>ant</u>

82 Underline the smallest of these words:

    elephant   hedgehog   <u>pig</u>   rabbit   goat   sheep   spider

83 Underline the middle-sized number:

    84735   87435   83475   83745   <u>84374</u>

84 Underline the middle one of these:

    21678   22568   <u>21568</u>   23451   22965

[85–90]
Here is a bar graph showing the numbers of boys and girls in each class in a school.

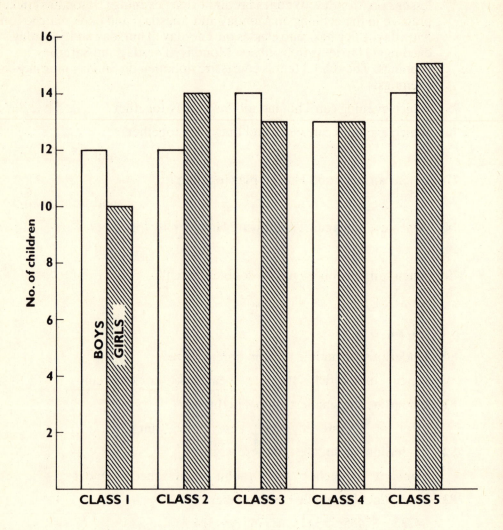

85 Which is the largest class? ....Class 5............
86 Which classes have more boys than girls? ....1 and 3............
87 Can you tell, quickly, approximately the average size of the classes in the school? ....26............
88 Again quickly, can you tell approximately how many children are in the school? ....130............
89 Are there as many boys as girls? The same number
90 Which class has the most room for extra girls? ....Class 1............

PAPER 11

[91–96]
If **a** = 8, **b** = 6, **c** = 4, **d** = 3 and **e** = 10, find the value of:

91 **a** + **b** − **c** = ...e......... Answer as a letter.

92 **a** × **b** = ...48......... Answer in figures.

93 $\dfrac{b + c}{e}$ = ...1......... Answer in figures.

94 **a** + **b** + **c** + **d** + **e** = ...31......... Answer in figures.

95 $\dfrac{a + b + c}{d}$ = ...b......... Answer as a letter.

96 $\dfrac{a \times b}{c \times d}$ = ...c......... Answer as a letter.

[97–100]
You go to school Monday to Friday each week and it costs you 30p each way in bus fares. A weekly bus pass would cost you £2.80, and a monthly bus pass (4 weeks) would cost £10.20.

97 How much would the weekly bus pass save you? ....20p each week.........

98 If you went back to the school for two evenings a week for rehearsals for the school play, how much would the weekly bus pass save you?
.........£1.40 each week.........

99 How much would you save each week if you had a monthly bus pass?
.........45p.........

100 How many days' school would you have to miss, because you were ill or on holiday, before you lost money on a monthly bus pass?
.........3 days.........

1. Which letter occurs twice in the word **stranger**? ...... r ......
2. Underline the correct word in the brackets to complete the sentence:
   Maria has a nephew whose name is (tall, rich, Julie, <u>Bruce</u>)
3. I bought three stamps which were 18p each, and gave the counter clerk a £1 coin. How much change should she give me? ...... 46p ......
4. John is three years younger than his brother David. David was born in 1974, so John was born in (1971, 1973, <u>1977</u>, 1877).

[5–14]
In each of these sets, cross out the word which means the opposite of the first word and ring the word which most nearly means the same:

5–6	fine	(smooth)	beautiful	~~coarse~~	course	thick
7–8	safe	sure	(secure)	danger	~~dangerous~~	shaky
9–10	bad	(rotten)	unripe	wicked	~~good~~	fresh
11–12	turbulent	(stormy)	rough	~~calm~~	placid	rippled
13–14	penniless	poor	(destitute)	~~wealthy~~	fat	opulent

[15–22]
If a word contains both letter **a** and letter **e**, put the number **1** after the word; if **a** but not **e** put **2**, if **e** but not **a** put **3**, if neither **a** nor **e** put **4**, and if either **a** or **e** comes twice put **5**.

15. gracious ...... 2 ......   16. able ...... 1 ......   17. canteen ...... 5 ......
18. grief ...... 3 ......   19. London ...... 4 ......   20. English ...... 3 ......
21. Spanish ...... 2 ......   22. European ...... 5 ......

PAPER 12

[23–34]
In the next examples, certain words are related to certain other words,

e.g. **hat** is to **head** as **glove** is to ....
Now **hat** goes on **head** and **glove** goes on **hand**, so the correct word to complete the sentence is **hand**.

hat is to **head** as **glove** is to **hand**
Complete the other sentences similarly:

23 **foot** is to **knee** as **hand** is to ......*elbow*......
24 **mare** is to **foal** as **ewe** is to ......*lamb*......
25 ......*feather*...... is to **bird** as **wool** is to **sheep**
26 **walk** is to ......*land*...... as **swim** is to **sea**
27 **up** is to **down** as **friend** is to ......*foe/enemy*......
28 **engine** is to ......*train*...... as **horse** is to **cart**
29 **engine** is to **petrol** as **horse** is to ......*hay/grass/fodder*......
30 **north** is to **south** as ......*warm*...... is to **cold**
31 **ant** is to **elephant** as **tiny** is to ......*enormous/huge*......
32 **happy** is to **sad** as **rejoice** is to ......*weep/grieve*......
33 **youth** is to ......*age*...... as **spring** is to **winter**
34 **cold** is to **ice** as **sweet** is to ......*sugar*......

[35–39]
Place the letters in the squares so that:

A is below one letter but above the rest.

B is above **C** and one other but below **D** and one other.

D and **E** are as far apart as possible.

There is only one letter in each square.

D
A
B
C
E

40 A ship sails 5 nautical miles north and 2 hours east, then 5 nautical miles south. It is now midnight. If it sails straight back to its starting point, what time will it arrive? ......*0200 hours*......

PAPER 12

[41–42]
In the sentence below, cross out the word that means the opposite of **gather**.

I saw the sower ~~scatter~~ the seeds.
How many times did the letter **s** appear in the above sentence?
The answer is three times this number. .... 15 ....

43 How many nines are there in 100? Write nothing but the answer.

100 contains ...... eleven ...... nines. 9 × 9 = ...

9 × 11 = ... remainder = ...

44 Draw a ring around the best answer to the question:
I eat ice cream because:
(a) It is nourishing   (b) It is expensive   (c) Everybody eats it
(d) It is nice   (e) (I like it)

45 Arrange the letters of the word **agriculture** in alphabetical order.

...... acegilrrtuu ......

46 Here is a word in which the letters are arranged in alphabetical order instead of in the usual way. What is the word?

ceilnp   ...... pencil ......

[47–64]
In each of the following sets you will find six words. One of the words tells you the kind of things most of the other words are and is called the "general word". Underline the general words.
There is also one word which does not easily fit in with all the others. Put a ring around the words that do not fit.

47–48	horse	cow	(friend)	donkey	lion	<u>animal</u>
49–50	<u>people</u>	soldiers	sailors	(dogs)	managers	zookeepers
51–52	cars	buses	<u>vehicles</u>	taxis	(police)	vans
53–54	Eiger	Everest	Snowdon	(Rhine)	<u>mountain</u>	Ben Nevis
55–56	English	Welsh	(American)	French	Spanish	<u>European</u>
57–58	rose	daisy	dandelion	<u>flowers</u>	(mistletoe)	poppy
59–60	<u>tool</u>	(nail)	hammer	saw	chisel	spade
61–62	eggs	<u>food</u>	bacon	bread	(bleach)	cake
63–64	run	walk	<u>move</u>	(sit)	hop	swim

[65–68]
In each sentence, cross out the part or parts of words necessary to make the sentence sensible:

65 David ordered ham~~lets~~ and eggs with his chip~~pings~~.
66 The library books were ~~subdued~~ back on the ~~thirty~~-second of the month.
67 They went to Wales for a short~~bread~~ weekend brea~~kfast~~.
68 He expects to arrive early, on the mo~~u~~rning train.

69 If one 10p piece weighs as much as two 5p pieces, which is the more valuable; 50 kg of 10p pieces or 100 kg of 5p pieces? *100 kg of 5p pieces*

70 Which is heavier, a litre of milk or a litre of cream taken from the same milk? *A litre of milk*

71 Hamish runs twice as far in 3 minutes as Susie runs in 1 minute, while Susie takes 1 minute to run as far as Alison runs in 2 minutes.

Who is the fastest runner? .... *Susie* ....

Who is the slowest runner? .... *Alison* ....

72 Which is the best answer? Underline your choice.
I go to the cinema because: (a) It only costs 80p
(b) I like the company   (c) <u>I like going</u>

[73–83]
Answer the following questions by writing **Yes, No** or **I don't know** as you think appropriate.

73 Is all ink black? .... *No*
74 Does the sun shine at night? .... *No*
75 Is a prince the son of a queen? .... *Yes*
76 Are all cooks women? .... *No*
77 Was Samson supposed to be a strong man? ..... *Yes*
78 Can ice be changed into steam? .... *Yes*
79 Are ships always made of material lighter than water? ..... *No*
80 Can a square have more than four sides? .... *No*
81 Are all good people famous? .... *No*
82 Are all famous people good? .... *No*
83 Can a sailing boat sail against the wind? .... *Yes*

PAPER 12

[84–91]
The top class in a school were set a project. It consisted of a survey of the pupils in the school to find out how they travelled to school. After questioning all the children they compiled the following table of their information:

	Class 5	Class 4	Class 3	Class 2	Class 1
Number of pupils	30	31	30	27	29
Number travelling to school:					
By bus	8	9	10	6	3
By bicycle	7	5	2	1	0
Walking	12	14	17	16	20
By other means e.g. driven by car, train	3	3	1	4	6

They presented their information to the rest of the school in some beautifully drawn pie charts but forgot to label the chart for each class. From the information in the table, can you decide which pie chart belongs to each class?

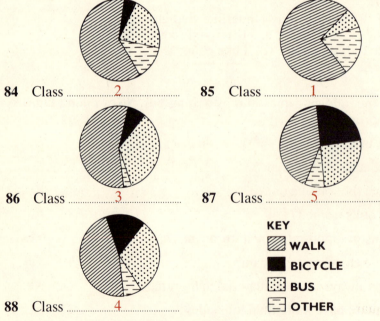

84 Class .... 2 ....
85 Class .... 1 ....
86 Class .... 3 ....
87 Class .... 5 ....
88 Class .... 4 ....

KEY
▨ WALK
■ BICYCLE
▦ BUS
▤ OTHER

89 Do more than half the children live within walking distance of the school?
.... Yes ....

90–91 From the patterns of travel to school, which would you think was the class with the oldest children? .... Class 5 ....
and why do you think so? .... More bicycles than any other class ....

[92–94]

I calculate that after paying the costs of owning my car it costs me 10p for every mile that I drive. There is a large supermarket 12 miles from home and a little corner shop which stocks most items within a hundred metres of my house. The cost of the goods in the supermarket is about 20% less than in the corner shop.

92 How much does it cost me to visit the supermarket? .... £2.40 ....

93 What value of goods will I need to buy from the supermarket to save the cost of using the car? .... £12 ....

94 How much would I save every week if I got all my grocery shopping in one visit to the supermarket instead of spending £60 at the corner shop?
.... £9.60 ....

[95–100]

I have brief instructions with my video tape recorder telling how to record from the television. Unfortunately the dog has chewed them up. Put them in the right order by writing the correct number in the sequence in the space after each instruction.

95 Press the record button on the front panel or the remote control. .... 6 ....

96 Reset the tape counter to 0000. .... 5 ....

97 Choose whether you want high quality recording or long play recording by setting the tape speed selector to SP or LP. .... 3 ....

98 Insert a blank video cassette in the machine. .... 4 ....

99 Make sure the timer record switch is set to "off" in case the timer is set to record immediately you switch on. .... 1 ....

100 Switch on the machine. .... 2 ....

Thomas Nelson and Sons Ltd
Nelson House   Mayfield Road
Walton-on-Thames   Surrey
KT12 5PL   UK

51 York Place
Edinburgh
EH1 3JD   UK

Thomas Nelson (Hong Kong) Ltd
Toppan Building 10/F
22A Westlands Road
Quarry Bay   Hong Kong

Distributed in Australia by

Thomas Nelson Australia
480 La Trobe Street
Melbourne   Victoria 3000
and in Sydney, Brisbane, Adelaide and Perth

First edition published by Thomas Nelson and Sons Ltd © H H Thomas 1951

This revised edition published by Thomas Nelson and Sons Ltd © A J Thomas 1988

ISBN 0-17-424481-9 } Pupils' Book   ISBN 0-17-424482-7 } Answer Book
NPN 98765432   NPN 98765432

Designed, illustrated and photoset by Gecko Limited, Bicester, Oxon
Printed in Great Britain by Ebenezer Baylis and Son Ltd, Worcester and London

All Rights Reserved. This publication is protected in the United Kingdom by the Copyright Act 1956 and in other countries by comparable legislation. No part of it may be reproduced or recorded by any means without the permission of the publisher. This prohibition extends (with certain very limited exceptions) to photocopying and similar processes, and written permission to make a copy or copies must therefore be obtained from the publisher in advance. It is advisable to consult the publisher if there is any doubt regarding the legality of any proposed copying.